JOB QUEST

How to Become the Insider Who Gets Hired

SHEILA MARKIN NIELSEN

Nielsen Career Press
CHICAGO

Chicago, IL
http://www.nielsencareerconsulting.com

Printed and bound in the United States of America.

Publisher's Cataloging-in-Publication data
Nielsen, Sheila Markin.
    Job quest : how to become the insider who gets hired / Sheila Markin Nielsen.
    p. cm.
    ISBN 978-0-692-37277-7
    Includes bibliographical references.

1. Job hunting. 2. Career development. 3. Vocational guidance. 4. Success. I. Title.

HF5382.7 .N542 2015
650.14 --dc23   2015901327

This book is dedicated to my husband, Art – you inspire me every day with your engagement in life, your love of learning and friendships, and your generous spirit. You are my soul mate. And our girls – it's great sharing the journey with you!

Table of Contents

Part III: Launch Your Quest

About the Author

SHEILA MARKIN NIELSEN IS A LEADER in the field of career counseling for lawyers and other professionals. She received her master's degree in social work from Bryn Mawr College in 1973 and her JD from Temple University School of Law in 1977. After law school, she worked as a criminal prosecutor, first as an assistant district attorney in Philadelphia, then as a state's attorney in Chicago, and then as an assistant U.S. attorney in Chicago until 1984.

In 1983, Ms. Nielsen helped create the Part-Time Lawyers Network of the Chicago Bar Association and chaired that group from 1984 to 1987. In 1988, she helped create a national association, Lawyers for Alternative Work Schedules, which she ran for two years.

In 1990, Ms. Nielsen developed her own career counseling and consulting service specializing in attorneys but also helping other professionals, Nielsen Career Consulting. For over twenty-five years, she has counseled and coached lawyers and other professionals who are dealing with a wide variety of career issues, including career path issues, job search issues, alternative work-time options, and career development. She provides guidance for clients who have difficult workplace problems, such as dealing with a difficult boss, learning to delegate, managing time, and marketing. She provides executive coaching assistance to many firms and companies. She also assists some mid- to large-size firms and companies with their outplacement needs.

In 1994, Ms. Nielsen received an award from the Part-Time Lawyers Network of the Chicago Bar Association. In 2001, she was honored with an Outstanding Alumni Leadership Award from Lake Forest College. She has contributed to the field of career counseling and coaching by writing over eighty columns and articles appearing in the *Chicago Bar Association Record, Illinois Legal Times, New York Law School Law Review, Legal Times of Washington DC (now the National Law Journal), Illinois Bar Journal, Detroit Legal News, Florida Bar Journal,* and many others. She has been an invited speaker over seventy times across the country at many conferences including American Bar Association (ABA), National Association of Women Lawyers (NAWL), National Association for Law Placement (NALP), and the Chicago Institute for Psychoanalysis, as well as many law schools and university alumni association meetings. She contributed to two ABA books for lawyers: *Breaking Traditions* and *Living with the Law.* She has done a number of continuing education webcasts and provided career advice on the LexisNexis website and ABA webinars. In 2011, the ABA published her book, *Job Quest for Lawyers: The Essential Guide to Finding and Landing the Job You Want.* That book was a best seller for the ABA and has enjoyed a five star rating from readers on Amazon. The basic concepts from that original book have been expanded and repurposed in this book for job seekers across a spectrum of fields.

Ms. Nielsen continues to speak nationwide on a variety of topics, including career direction, job search, marketing, leadership, career success, interviewing, time management, alternative work-time options, and many other topics.

Acknowledgments

THIS BOOK WAS CONCEIVED over a bottomless cup of coffee and a stack of powdered sugar-dusted banana pancakes at The Original Pancake House, where my childhood friend, Mary Trimble, insisted that I had to birth a book with this information for job seekers.

When we were in junior high, Mary and I used to walk from our homes near the Northwestern University campus out to the large jumbled rocks piled along the edge of Lake Michigan. There we sat for hours, watching the waves, talking and wondering about what would happen in our lives. Mary was a gifted poet. She had to write. I was a dancer. I had to move.

Some forty years and many career incarnations later, we rediscovered our friendship. By then, both of us had had three kids, been divorced, and rediscovered love with new guys. As predicted, Mary had become a writer. In my career I had evolved: from dancer to social worker to lawyer to career counselor. As predicted, I had to move.

Now in the middle of busy lives, we caught up when we could over pancake breakfasts. It was during one of these breakfasts that Mary insisted I write a book. She had been listening to me describe what I teach my clients about networking for a job, and encouraged me with enthusiasm to get the message out to a wider audience.

Mary has been muse, cheerleader, videographer, editor, and therapist during this journey. She and her colleague, Michael Bai, produced a

3

wonderful DVD that contains key concepts of the Job Quest. Thank you, Mary, for your pesky insistence. I am very grateful.

I also owe a huge thank you to my husband, Art, the love of my life, who is also my muse, cheerleader, editor, and therapist. His encouragement has been crucial through the many twists and turns of this trek to publication. Enthusiastic, passionate, determined, insightful, engaging, and intelligent, he is a true helpmate and my best friend. His faith in this project has been essential.

Another shout out goes to our three kids, Jeni, Katy, and Cindy. All of them sat through many years of many dinners, hearing me talk about and work out the concepts in this book. Apparently they were actually listening, as evidenced by their own various challenging and ultimately successful job quests. They have also been very supportive of their fourth sibling: this time-consuming literary progeny.

My father-in-law, A.C. Nielsen of the Nielsen ratings, deserves a big thank-you. His knowledge of the business world, especially the way employers think about job creation and job seekers, has been invaluable. His steadfast encouragement and support were immensely helpful to me when he was alive.

My sister, Wendy, has been a well-spring of sustenance. I could not have made it these past years without our many talks. She has helped my inner gyroscope back to center time and time again.

I thank my mother, a natural networker who taught me so much about being a true friend. She cared about everyone – taxi drivers, shopkeepers, neighbors, and strangers in need. Her friends and family had the benefit of her generous spirit. Unafraid to quietly think and act outside the box, she wore unique apparel when it pleased her, even when her children were appalled, and always remembered to watch the sun set in the vast sky, feel the wind, and really listen to the sound of the chimes. I wish she were alive to enjoy this book; it embodies many of the concepts she knew and used in her life.

I thank my father, who was both a brilliant and visionary electrical engineer who conceived of and built the first flat panel TVs. Also an accomplished pianist and teacher, Dad worked hard to be the best he could be at every endeavor, and was a model of perseverance. He was also my early role model as the unofficial career counselor for our extended family. Many of our relatives and quite a few of his piano students came to him for career advice. Dad and I talked about their decisions, and thought through ways to help them make the best choices for their futures.

I also want to thank the wonderful people who have helped me repurpose the original book and turn it into the new book that is a guide for job seekers generally, especially professionals and new graduates. Jeanne Follman has been a wonderful editor and source of excellent information and guidance throughout this process. And thanks to Brian Judkins we now have a vibrant and clever Map of the Quest! Mary Trimble has continued to supply her thoughtful and knowledgeable support and guidance as well. And Jill McCall, you were the catalyst that got this new book into production. Thank you all so much! Thank you also to Gretchen Quillan for her excellent copy editing and to Monica Thomas of TLC Graphics for the engaging book cover design. And I am delighted to collaborate with PR by the Book.

Finally, I want to thank the many gifted networkers I have had the good fortune to counsel. They have taught me a great deal about what works and what doesn't work in a job search. I am indebted to them for their trust in me and for their many valuable insights.

Introduction: A Surprising Epiphany about How People Really Get Jobs

How do people find jobs? How do people **really** find jobs? Did you ever ask your friends that question? Chances are if you ask your friends, "How did you land your job?" you are likely to hear this answer: "I got lucky. It was chance." When I first began my career counseling business for lawyers over twenty-five years ago, I decided to ask many of my friends who had conducted successful job searches how they got their jobs so I could learn how to help my future clients. Over and over I heard: "I got lucky. I was in the right place at the right time."

This was not the answer I had been hoping to hear. I thought my friends' responses would help me understand the way people network effectively to land job opportunities. I had hoped to learn useful job search strategies and ways to create winning résumés or cover letters and great ideas for hearing about jobs so I could share that knowledge with my future clients, who were looking for jobs and having trouble finding them. When people said they got lucky, it sounded like they found a job by sheer dumb luck, or mere chance, as if they had tripped over a job and "Wow, wasn't that great for me!" What was I supposed to tell my clients? "After you leave my office I hope you go out into the big world and just get lucky somehow" sounded like the worst advice imaginable.

I began counseling people in 1990 and very quickly I could see that some of my clients were gifted, natural networkers, and others were struggling with the whole business of networking for job opportunities. One of the fun things about being a career counselor is that I could ask nosy, probing questions about job searches and get honest answers from my clients. If someone said, "I got lucky finding this job," I could say, "What exactly made you so lucky? Who did you know? How did you get to know that person? What exactly did you say to that person? And what did that conversation open up for you?" As I worked with hundreds of clients and as I learned from the hundreds of work histories they shared with me, I could see patterns and strategies that were helping the gifted, natural networkers open up more opportunities and options as they looked for jobs.

I began to realize that the "insiders" were getting the jobs. People known and trusted by a workplace were enjoying a great advantage. This is true now and it has been true in the past. It makes sense that someone known and trusted will have an edge. But what I learned from the gifted networkers was something more important: namely, that it is possible to create more job opportunities by engaging in a process of rapid relationship and trust building in the field or industry where you are trying to find work. The advantage comes from a process the gifted networkers engaged in where they were seeking information using the right messaging while also giving back to others and being generous and authentically engaged and active in the industry or realm where they were looking for work.

This was a surprising epiphany, because after reading many books and articles about job search, I originally believed that most people got their jobs by answering ads and sending out cover letters. In fairness, some people do, in fact, find jobs that way. But more people find opportunities through connecting with others. The search can be productive and remarkably quick if it consists of building relationships in an effective way, and at times being bold, creative, and crafty about engineering opportunities to open doors. Although in the beginning of my practice I had trouble believing that the fastest way to a new job was through rapid relationship and trust building, over time I became convinced and incorporated it into my practice. I felt that my clients who were struggling should have the advantage of knowing this important information about how to search for jobs. I wanted them to have a level playing field with the natural networkers.

I created a job search training session for my clients to teach them how to develop opportunities using this search method and then coached them in their efforts. I created a blueprint for them, and I also used the analogy of a quest to help them understand what they should be trying to do and who they needed to seek out. This approach was very effective. For many of my clients, it was a game changer. This information changed their job searches into something they truly enjoyed doing, where they had dreaded it before. It was the best way to overcome the problem of being an unknown outsider trying to penetrate a workplace that favors insiders. I learned that just as people can improve their golf game or their tennis game, job seekers can improve their relationship-developing skills with good information and coaching.

I now understand much more about how luck and chance figure into job searches. After counseling and coaching more than three thousand clients over a period of more than twenty-five years, I have learned that luck and chance *do* play an important role in job searches, but there is a reason for that. From my client's experiences searching for work, I've learned who gets luckier and why.

Lucky job seekers are able to create more good fortune for themselves, sometimes defying the odds when it comes to landing the jobs they want. These job seekers are connecting in the right way – and ultimately being endorsed by – people who are known and trusted by a workplace because these people have actually have met the job seeker and are impressed by what they experience in that in-person meeting, which is really an interview, whether it is termed that or not. Lucky job seekers set their goals and then set about their mission to find work: doing research, engaging with other people in a particularly productive way, enlisting their help by using the right messaging and advocating for themselves effectively, eliciting information, overcoming barriers to success, and creating authentic friendships, as well as giving back to the people they encounter in the realm where they are searching. In short, many lucky job seekers are engineering success by coming to the attention of a workplace through rapid relationship and trust building, endorsed by a trusted contact who is known and credible to the workplace. Surprisingly, many of these natural networkers do not seem to understand or realize how effective they are compared to typical job seekers. When questioned about how they landed their jobs, many are unaware of the strategies they employed to create these job opportunities. They often give the standard response: "It was chance. I was in the right place at the right time."

As my counseling practice evolved, I realized that I needed to share concepts and approaches I learned from my "lucky" clients with all of my clients, even the good networkers, because they needed to understand how the good fortune they created could be replicated in any future job search. The search method and training session that I used with clients became a presentation and then the book, *Job Quest for Lawyers* which was published by the American Bar Association in 2011. Learning the job quest method is the fastest way to change job search fortune. In this book, I have expanded and repurposed my job quest method for the professional job seeker and new graduate.

In my own life, I have had my share of difficult job search quests. After law school, I was determined to become a prosecutor. I had gone to Temple Law School in Philadelphia, and I wanted to become a district attorney (DA) in Philadelphia. My friends, new graduates of Temple Law School who had recently been hired by that office, told me that I needed a personal connection higher up than they were to have a chance to be interviewed. I had no relatives or friends that I knew of who could connect me to the DA's office. But I found a way to get hired there.

After moving to Chicago from Philadelphia, I needed a part-time job while I studied for the bar exam. There seemed to be no way to find a part-time job as a lawyer. There were no ads in the local *Daily Law Bulletin* or part-time jobs listed in career resource centers at law schools. But after three days of looking for work, I was able to create a part-time position for myself with a wonderful matrimonial lawyer in town.

I was told that it was unlikely that anyone without a connection would land a job at the state's attorney's office in Cook County. I had no connection there, but I landed that job as well.

And finally, many well-meaning people told me that I was a long shot for a position as an assistant United States attorney, even though I was an assistant state's attorney with ample trial experience in state court at the time I applied for that position. There were hundreds of outstanding applicants for a few positions. I did not graduate from a top ten school. My two worst subjects in law school were criminal law and constitutional law. I had not worked as a law clerk for a federal judge. I was cautioned not to get my hopes up. People like me didn't get to be assistant U.S. attorneys. But I did.

For many years whenever people asked me how I got those jobs, I would tell them that I got lucky, and I believed that. But after years of working as a career counselor and watching and guiding thousands of job seekers, as well as hearing hundreds of work histories from clients talking about how they had gotten their jobs, I realized that I made a lot of that luck happen, just as the gifted networkers in my practice were doing. At the time I conducted those early job searches, I was not aware of what I was doing or how I was getting the result I wanted. Today I am acutely aware of the process of making good luck happen, and I teach these strategies to my clients as I coach them through their job searches. I wrote this book to share these strategies and the job quest method with you.

My own experience and the experiences of my gifted clients form the basis for this book. This book contains the job quest method and the collective wisdom of many job seekers whose names have been changed but whose stories are true. They have found their way to good opportunities using the approach you will learn here. I hope it helps you, too.

Let's begin.

Part I

The Basics

Where you learn about the insider advantage, what luck has to do with it, how fortune favors the prepared mind, and review a blueprint for the quest.

Chapter One:
The Insider Advantage

You need to find a job. You have to look for opportunities. You are totally ready to do this, but you are not sure how to start. There are jobs posted on the Internet. It makes sense to go there and start applying. That's what everyone does to find work, right? So that is what you do.

You jump into it starting with sites, such as Monster, Indeed, Career Builder, and Craig's List. You look at the postings. You find jobs that are in your field and some others you would like to interview for even though your skills are not a perfect match. If you could just get a chance to talk with someone at the workplace, you know you could make a good case!

You apply. You send out résumés and cover letters, and you hope. And you apply to some more postings and hope. And then … and then … sometimes nothing. It seems like you sent your résumé to a black hole. Sometimes you get an interview over the phone and then … nothing. And sometimes you get a phone interview followed by an in-person interview, and maybe a series of tests, and more in-person interviews, and then … and then … a rejection. What happened? What is going on here? Who is getting hired anyhow?

Peter Cappelli, Professor of Management at The Wharton School and director of Wharton's Center for Human Resources writes about the problem of hiring people using software and online automated systems and how that elimination of the human interface is resulting in good people not being able to get jobs that could be good matches. His book, *Why Good People Can't Get Jobs*, is a must-read for anyone trying to understand why sending a résumé to a workplace using an automated system can be an exercise in frustration. Cappelli writes, "Because job applications are done online, applicants rarely talk to anyone, even by e-mail, during the hiring process."

In Cappelli's book, Elaine Orler of Talent Function describes how automated systems work. "First, hiring managers write up descriptions of the job they need to fill. Since hiring managers frequently cannot agree on exactly what they want, the description ends up being vague, a practice that inevitably encourages still more people to apply for the position."

Cappelli notes that there is already a huge pool of job seekers, which is overwhelming human resources departments that are supposed to keep costs down. This results in further automation of the entire hiring process. In addition, federal antidiscrimination regulations can result in a description of qualifying requirements that are very broad in order to avoid the appearance of discrimination, which encourages still more people to apply. To add to the problem, "Managers pile all the credentials and expertise into the job description to minimize the risk that the candidate will fail (be an imperfect match for the skill set sought), making it virtually impossible to find anyone who fits." Cappelli notes that Tom Keebler at the HR consulting firm Towers Watson, who consults with employers about their hiring systems, says "even well-intentioned hiring managers have a problem trying to identify skills that are not easily associated with credentials or experience." And once the requirement is part of the software, it becomes a "hurdle that applicants have to clear to become a qualified candidate."

According to Jacquelyn Smith in her *Forbes Online* article "7 Things You Probably Didn't Know About Your Job Search," fifty percent of applicants are weeded out before anyone looks at them. In his book, Cappelli illustrates the problem with examples of people who are unquestionably qualified for a position, yet are rejected by the software program because the particular brand name being sought in the job description was different from the one used in the résumé or a title was different in the résumé from the one used in the software. Cappelli notes that software cannot "lean back in a chair opposite the job seeker and iron out these little misunderstandings over a cup of coffee."

It turns out you only have a small chance of getting a job through an external online source, according to Gerry Crispin of *CareerXroads*, an author of the annual "Source of Hire Report." Having an internal company contact is far more effective than applying for jobs using job boards like Monster, Career Builder or Craig's List. Indeed it is the most successful external source compared to the other options, as Jacquelyn Smith describes in her *Forbes Online* article "New Research Shows Where Employers Find Their New Hires." How ineffective is the application using a large search engine? The literature supports the fact that finding a job using an online site has a very low probability of success – somewhere in the range of 2.1 to 4 percent – and that internal referrals are by far the most effective sources used by workplaces to find their hires.

Think of the job market as a big, messy, open marketplace that is constantly shifting and changing. It is full of intrigue and politics. Who has the real power to hire? Who has the client's business? It is buffeted by the economy. Should the company hire now or wait? Is the big client going to stay or leave for another firm with lower rates or a closer relationship with a key person? When a company or organization posts a job opening is that a real job or is it bogus because they actually have a good person inside the workplace or someone who came highly recommended and who probably has the inside track but they want to avoid the appearance of favoritism?

In my work with clients, I hear about these behind-the-scenes activities. For example, a client I was working with recently did an excellent job of relationship building and went through a thorough interview process. He was promised the job by the employer, but workplace protocol required that the company post a job description online. My client expressed concern that the workplace might not hire him after all, but the person in charge of hiring assured him he should not worry, the job would be his, the job posting was really just required by agency protocol. Then another client of mine saw that posting and came to work with me to try to put together the best possible résumé and cover letter because he knew he was perfect for this job. Of course the job was landed by the client who had built the internal relationships and gotten the promise from the employer.

A job posting may look like a clear cut recitation of skills that the company seeks, but behind that posting could be a great deal of uncertainty and even a mistaken emphasis on certain skills. Hard skills can be identified, but what about soft skills? Soft skills are often very important but they are hard to describe and rarely make it into the posting. You will never see a job description like this: "We need someone who has amazing people skills to work with our ridiculously difficult clients and can also get along with the overbearing manager in this group who has demoralized everyone who ever worked with him."

Furthermore, a workplace might not officially be considering additional staff, but if the right person shows up at the door, she might be hired because the work is there and the skill set is a match and the person has come to the attention of the workplace with a glowing recommendation from someone known and trusted. Bingo. And there was never a posting. Or maybe there was a posting, and maybe that posting was even generated after the candidate was discovered, but the person in charge of hiring had already made up her mind. The posting was more for show.

Postings are merely the tip of the iceberg when it comes to jobs. About 80% of available jobs are never advertised, according to Jacquelyn Smith in her *Forbes Online* article "7 Things You Probably Didn't Know About Your Job Search." Many workplaces need help but do not post or have not yet posted a job. If they need to hire and if the right candidate can show up on the radar screen, that person might well get lucky.

Given the chaotic, messy nature of the job market and the difficulty getting past the many hurdles that are set up by the workplace and particularly the software systems being used to do the early vetting of candidates, how are you supposed to find a job? How are you going to prove that you have the right skills and abilities and would be a great addition when a workplace is unapproachable?

The Bureau of Labor Statistics estimates that 70% of jobs are found by networking. This number is reported in the Job Openings and Labor Turnover Survey, or JOLTS. JOLTS data also reveals that 40% of jobs filled by employers are never advertised. "Once we include the number of jobs that were filled by someone known to the employer, the number soars to 70%," says Kimberly Beatty in her *Jobfully Online Content and Marketing* blog post titled "The Math Behind the Networking Claim."

Networking seems to be the search method of choice, but networking is not defined very well. What is networking? Most people think networking consists of asking everyone you know if they have heard of a job or opportunity in your industry and seeing if they can come up with a good match or some suggestions about where to look. Many clients I work with have been networking in this way. I call it *networking as usual*. If there is low hanging fruit and the contact person really understands the jobseeker's background and skills, this approach might be helpful. But many of the clients I work with have already tried networking in this way and they tell me they are not landing jobs using this approach. They think that networking doesn't work for them.

Have you ever had someone ask you if you have heard of a job in their industry? Your response is likely to be, "No, I haven't heard of anything but I will keep an eye out for you and I will call or e-mail you if I do hear of something." End of conversation. The truth is that even really nice, helpful people do not want to spend time hunting for a job for you. And the default thinking is something like this: "I hope he finds a new job but I don't have the time to look for him. I am sure he will find something one of these days. Meantime, I hope he doesn't become a pest, calling me up and asking more of me. I am just too busy!"

Let's look a little more closely at who lands the jobs. Silk Road, a talent manager solutions provider, recently reported that internal sources produce the most hires. Internal sources included employee referrals, company website, current employees, and recruiter-sourced referrals. Employee referrals resulted in 61% of the hires. The company website resulted in 26% of the hires. Current employees accounted for 8% of the hires. Former employees were 2%. Recruiter-sourced was 2%. Walk-ins were 1%. The Silk Road findings in the report titled "Recruitment Marketing Effectiveness: Meaningful Metrics Straight from the Source," reveal that internal sources produce almost twice the number of hires as external ones, which include job search engines, job boards, print advertising, and job fairs. "It is still about who you know. It shouldn't be a surprise to anyone that employee referrals are the number one source; those candidates come with built-in recommendations and in many cases have already been sold on your culture and know more about your company than the average external candidate," says Thomas Boyle, director of product marketing at Silk Road, as quoted by Jacquelyn Smith in her *Forbes Online* article "New Research Shows Where Employers Find Their New Hires."

The insider advantage is a big advantage. But here is the quandary you face if you don't have an inside track: how are you supposed to become known and trusted by a workplace that will not even respond to your carefully crafted résumé and cover letter? How can you make your case to an impenetrable workplace that will not allow you to come in and meet with them for an interview even though your skills and background and personality are a great match?

The answer can be found by understanding the way the gifted, natural networkers create good luck and open doors for themselves.

We need to talk about good luck and how luck gets created.

We need to talk about the way fortune favors the prepared mind and how to prepare the mind for a job quest.

We need to talk about how to go on a job quest.

We need to talk about the map of the quest, a blueprint to guide your search efforts.

We need to be sure you are well-prepared for the journey with the right tools, supplies, and messaging in your informal or formal interviews for a successful result.

And we need to talk about some overarching concepts that you will want to use as you conduct your search.

It is important to start by understanding how luck works and how it can be created.

Chapter Two: What Does Luck Have to Do with It?

When you ask people how they got their jobs you often hear, "I got lucky." Maybe you think "How did that luck really happen? What made that person so lucky? Who did they know?" Those were just some of the questions I wanted to ask lucky job seekers. And when I became a career counselor I got to ask those questions and probe more deeply the ways some people create job search luck. The answers may surprise you.

I BEGAN MY CAREER COUNSELING BUSINESS in 1990, and after a few years of probing and learning from my clients and my friends, I could clearly see that luck does play a role in getting opportunities in life, including jobs, and that the luck is not **dumb** luck. It is not as if successful job finders trip over jobs, but more that certain attitudes and ways of interacting with people and interfacing with the world create good fortune.

This is consistent with the findings of Richard Wiseman, a Scottish psychologist who has studied self-reported lucky and unlucky people. Wiseman has written a book entitled, *The Luck Factor: The Four Essential Principles*. He began his study by putting an ad in a number of newspapers and magazines asking people who considered themselves to be naturally lucky people to answer the ad and become part of his research study. He also invited people who thought of themselves as naturally unlucky in life to answer the ad. He then had a group of self-reported lucky and self-reported unlucky people to study. He subjected both groups of people to a series of tests, activities, and experiments to learn about what contributes to luck in life. He learned that the so-called lucky people did not predict the lottery any better than the unlucky group, but they were, in fact, having better lives. They were getting opportunities and chances in life that the unlucky people were not. They were marrying the people they wanted to marry. They were landing the jobs they wanted.

After Wiseman had studied the two groups for about three years, observing how they behaved in different settings and circumstances, he was able to conclude that the difference between the two groups was a difference in mindset. Lucky people have four ways of thinking that contribute to good fortune.

- Lucky people are **open** to chance opportunities.
- Lucky people are aware, alert, and **observant**. You could say they have good intuitive judgment.
- Lucky people are more **optimistic**. They have a glass half-full mentality.
- Lucky people are **resilient** and find treasure in the trash.

In his book, *The Luck Factor: The Four Essential Principles*, Wiseman describes a behavioral experiment that helps to illustrate how luck gets created in life. In the experiment, Wiseman set up a coffeehouse with cameras on the inside and the outside. He placed people in the coffeehouse (actors) who were ready to talk and provide information if they were approached, and he also put a five pound note on the threshold of the coffeehouse door. With cameras rolling, he observed people from each group of lucky and unlucky individuals as they entered the scene to see how they would behave.

Martin from the lucky group is an example of how a typical "lucky" person behaves in this setting. As he enters the shop he sees the five pound note on the ground (he is aware, alert, observant), and he picks it up, probably thinking to himself, "Wow, more evidence that I am a lucky person!" But the next thing he does is what actually makes him lucky. He sits down at the coffee bar next to another guy and says, "I just found some money lying on the ground by the door, and I would like to buy you a cup of coffee." Notice that he gives the other person a gift and interacts with him. They talk together. Because of his openness and generosity, you can see that Martin is going to do well in terms of his access to information and potential opportunity.

Brenda is the example from the unlucky group. She enters the same coffeehouse but she misses the five pound note at the threshold of the door. It is likely that she is anxious, or self-absorbed, and not as aware, alert, and observant as Martin was. She sits by herself and orders a cup of coffee, drinks it, and leaves without interacting with anyone other than the barista taking her order. Brenda had the same potential as Martin, but she did not maximize that potential. Her chances for creating opportunities are not going to be as great as Martin's.

This illustration shows us how luck gets created by people with some of the elements that boost opportunity, such as being open to experience, having reliable intuitive judgment, and maintaining positive expectations.

When it comes to job search luck, we need to add four more elements for a lucky job seeker. These elements are 1. pragmatism, 2. tenacity, 3. opportunism, and 4. generosity. They make a difference when you have to work your way toward a goal. When you are looking for a job it works best to identify your end goal, namely the career/field/industry and the more specific type of job you are looking for. Then you can work your way to your goal. You want to figure out your career goal first because you do not want to be wandering around hoping to bump into the right industry or job. That is what many people do, unfortunately. Instead of planning first, they drift into a career based on comments made by well-intentioned people, or hopes or even directives from parents or friends who may not know enough about the person and the career match. Often job seekers just hope their career choices will work out for the best.

Job seekers fall into this mode of hopeful wandering because they do not know how to predict or make good educated guesses about which career paths will be the best choices for them. Though not generally part of the academic curriculum, this would be a helpful class for people in high school and college. Career choice is arguably one of the most important decisions you will make in your life. Yet many people are unsure how to figure out the right career direction. To have good job search luck, you want to figure out the career path you seek based on a clear-eyed assessment of your personal strengths and needs. You want to do this before setting out on the journey. And when you do that assessment, set your career goal and then understand how to work toward it, your good fortune is greater. (See Appendices for Assessment Tools to help you figure out your career direction.) So what do we need to add to the job search mindset?

Wiseman talks about optimism, and that is a valuable attitude to have for job search, but a job seeker also has to be realistic. So, the first additional element to add is **pragmatism**. There are books and articles that claim you should do what you love and everything will work out for the best. But in a job search, you need to be very knowledgeable not only about what you want to be doing in your career to be happy and satisfied, but where you fit into the marketplace as well. You want to be sure you are positioning yourself to be valuable, skilled, and good at what you do or what you want to do in the future. You have to have the expertise that the employer is looking for if you hope to be hired. There are exceptions, but the majority of hires are based in large part on the current skill set applicants bring to the table. Even if you have a well-connected friend or family member who gets you a job based on their connections (yes, that can happen), without the necessary skill set for the job, you are not likely to last in that position. It is important to be pragmatic.

Second, you need to be able to follow through or "work your quest." In a job search, you set a goal and if you are networking productively, it feels as if you are working your way toward that goal, not meandering around, lost in the woods. Call it **tenacity**. You want to move toward a job or career goal that plays to your personal strengths and where you know there is market activity or workflow. You may need to start out with internships and apprenticeships and coursework, then move to starter jobs that are basic and not very challenging but where you learn more about the field or workplace and develop skills. Job search tenacity is the ability to follow through with the tasks that get you to your goal.

The third additional mindset element is something I term **opportunism**. This is specifically what I see the more gifted, natural networkers doing. It consists of three elements: first, an **adventurous attitude** in which these networkers think, "You never know. I think I will try this or try that. Maybe it will get me closer to my goal." Second, and coupled with this attitude, they become **good researchers** who want to learn about key people in the field and, third, they find a way to **connect with** or meet up with key people but not in an aggressive or pesky way. It can feel a bit like stalking, but actually it is just good research and creative engineering to meet up with helpful people.

The fourth additional element is **generosity**. The person you connect with should be better off for having met you. If you can give to others and make their lives a bit better, they will return the favor if they can. It is remarkable how much this mindset matters in a job search and how well others can tell if you are genuine, credible and authentic when you connect with them.

The four attitudes I'd add to Wiseman's mindset of being open, observant, optimistic, and resilient are pragmatism, tenacity, opportunism, and generosity. They all work together to move the job seeker closer to his or her goals. But how do they work? To use these ideas in an effective job search, we need to understand more specifically how luck gets created in a job search. Knowledge and preparation enhance good fortune.

Chapter Three: Fortune Favors the Prepared Mind

When it comes to good luck, Louis Pasteur once said, "Fortune favors the prepared mind." He was referring to the many lucky discoveries that occur in science. Teflon, penicillin, and many other discoveries seemingly occurred by chance. But when you look a little closer, you can see that good fortune happened because the person making the discovery was knowledgeable about the field. Good luck happens within a context that starts with good information.

ANOTHER RECENT CHANCE DISCOVERY points to the important concept of fortune favoring the prepared mind for job seekers. That discovery was graphene. A group of scientists were trying to develop an extremely thin electronic superconductor that could be used to create more compact cell phones and iPads and other devices. The approach they were using was to shave down a block of lead (think: pencil lead) and try to make it thinner and thinner. The way they attempted to do this was to apply adhesive strips (think: scotch tape) and pull off layer after layer of material. This approach seemed to be the right one, but it was not yielding the thin material they were looking for because the material kept breaking. One day, two of the scientists working on this project had a brainstorm. What if they were throwing away the super thin superconductor they were looking for because it was on the discarded adhesive strips? And sure enough, that was the moment of discovery. There it was on the tape, the graphene they had been looking for! They were awarded the Nobel Prize for the discovery.

Have you ever put scotch tape on pencil lead and pulled it off? Graphene is invisible to the eye. You threw away that scotch tape. You didn't get the Nobel Prize. But if you had known what you were looking for, you might have discovered the next generation of material that will open the doors to the electronics of the future. How would you know that you had graphene on that tape unless you understood the underlying science? Fortune favors the prepared mind.

I like graphene as an image of lost opportunity. When you are well-informed, you can and often do see more, discover more, and open possibilities that other people miss. If you are not well-informed, you can miss even obvious possibilities.

When it comes to job search, there is a lot of missed graphene because people do not know what to look for or how to assess the potential. Let's go back to the way that most people conduct their networking searches and see what is getting missed.

Most people start with the "J" word. They ask everyone they know if they have heard of jobs in the field or industry. The typical answer is that they don't know of any jobs but will contact the job seeker if they hear of something. End of conversation. When you use the "J" word too soon, you miss out on some very important job search graphene.

1. **Your conversation is too short.** Long, gossipy, rumor-filled conversations are essential to a good search because they teach you the lay of the land and help you to tap into the on-the-ground information on the street. Where are the workplaces that might be interested in hiring a person with your skills? Where are the people you could connect with – in person – who might assist you?

2. **You do not advance your market knowledge.** You do not learn about places that are busy, active, and growing. You miss information about workflow.

3. **You do not create or deepen a friendship.** It turns out that friendship is very valuable for your search. Making other people's lives better and helping others even in small ways is

important. Just getting to know someone casually and being a good person is an important part of good relationship and trust building.

4. **You do not create trust.** Trust is huge in job searches. It is created in person, not remotely, through conversations over time.

5. **You get the "leper effect."** When you ask people to look for jobs for you, they will not spend their time doing that. Even really nice people will not do that for you. And they will feel guilty that they are not able to help you, so when you contact them again, they will likely keep you at arm's length. Since good networking is all about friendship and trust, you have put yourself at a decided disadvantage by using the "J" word too soon.

There does come a time in a job search when you can use the "J" word, but it is after you have done your homework and learned more about the market and applied the Formula for Getting Hired, which we will learn about in Chapter Five: How to Prepare for Your Quest.

Part of preparing your mindset for a productive job search has to do with some basic overarching ways of thinking about the search. Attitudes matter. Mindset matters. Even the way you conceptualize your role matters.

Most people think about job search as if they are using a toolbox approach. Open the box and try different tools. One day they might try answering job postings on Indeed. The next day they might contact recruiters. The next tool might be posting a résumé on LinkedIn. After that, maybe they will try a job fair. There is nothing wrong with trying a variety of approaches to the market, but if you shift the way you conceptualize your role, it can add to your good fortune. What is the best way to think about your search and your role in that search?

Think of your job search as a quest. It is an epic adventure and you are the protagonist of the yet-to-be created story. You are the star of the show. Your ability to engage with others, use humor, be clever and strategic, give back to people who help you, and really use all of yourself in this journey will make the difference in your success. The best approach to a job quest is to treat it like a game with a gamer's mentality: eager, engaged, adventurous, bold, persistent, aware, strategic, and intuitive. When you think of a gamer, eyes glued to the screen, keenly aware of how the game works, intently working the controls, and deeply involved – that is the right attitude to bring to your search. Or think Luke Skywalker and Princess Leia and their quest to overcome the evil Empire. Think Wizard of Oz. Think Siddhartha. Use whatever quest analogy works for you. For purposes of this book, we will use a medieval quest analogy.

You will be venturing out from the safety of your cottage and getting into the forest where you will be looking for wizards and knights and dealing with an occasional ogre. You will be trying to find your way to the right realm and the right castles and evading or outsmarting the dragons that guard the castle door. You will be doing good deeds and helping people. And when you create the opportunity to meet in person with wizards and knights, you will be ready with good messaging and advocacy and know how to have a masterful in-person meeting that will create better luck and good fortune.

Chapter Four:
Blueprint for the Quest

A productive job search is a journey from your current situation to the job you want. Your attitude matters a great deal. Relationship building and trust building is the best way to proceed. But what should you envision to help you to have a productive search? Think about your search as a quest, a medieval quest. You are the hero of this adventure. Your determination and tenacity, your energy and effort, your creativity and willingness to help others, even your sense of humor will make the difference in your ultimate success.

You are here: The Hero at the beginning of the Quest

This quest begins in your medieval *cottage* (your current situation/home/base of operations). There you are with your computer, working on your résumé, searching for and responding to job postings online. If you have been looking for a while, you are probably frustrated because you have been getting very little result for your effort.

You have probably sent your résumé and cover letters to a lot of *castles* (workplaces) by now, but you have not gotten an interview or you have been interviewed by phone and then dropped. You are getting worried and even a little depressed. What can you do to find a job if no one will even respond to your applications?

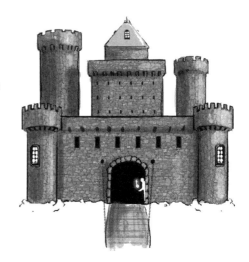

Frustrated, you leave the cottage to go outside for a break. In the distance beyond a clearing, you can see a forest and mountains, but you cannot see what lies beyond. How will you ever find a job when you cannot even see what's on the other side? The task of trying to figure out what is happening on the other side of the mountain seems overwhelming. You are tempted to go back inside, sit in front of your computer, and click on other castles' job postings. It may feel safer to answer ads all day long, but if you do that, you will encounter a serious and recurring problem.

You learn the challenges of the job search quest (dragons protect the castle!)

Medieval castles are notoriously well-defended, and these workplaces are no exception. They have moats, drawbridges, and a fire-breathing *dragon* (software scanners or other screening agents) stationed at the drawbridge to protect the castle from the advances of the horde of job seekers who are eager to have an interview.

The *keeper of the castle keys* or **key keeper** (the person who has the final say about who will be hired) is the one person who has the true power to give you a job, but your résumé will not be presented directly to the key keeper if you send it through cyberspace.

+ The key keeper is hidden away in the castle to avoid detection by the mob of job seekers beyond the castle walls.

- When you send your résumé to the castle, it is delivered directly to the dragon.
- The dragon does not want to let you in.
- In fact, the dragon has strict instructions to find fault with your résumé and will try hard to find some reason to throw it in the moat or incinerate it in a blast of fiery breath.
- The key keeper is a very busy person who has hired the dragon to ensure only the most qualified candidates make it into the inner sanctum of the castle for the in-person interview.

However, if you do your quest well, you may be able to avoid or outsmart the dragon. If you cannot avoid the dragon altogether, you will have people assisting you, your ***knights and wizards*** (helpful people), who will limit the dragon's ability to prevent you from entering the castle to meet the key keeper and other castle staff by shepherding your résumé past the dragon.

As we proceed, you will learn about these natural counselors and how to find and talk with them.

There are also castles that do not have dragons at the front drawbridge and may, in fact, welcome you into the castle for a conversation. They tend to be the smaller to midsize workplaces.

As with most heroic quests, this one requires some bravery and some creativity.

You will have to:

- Leave the safety of your cottage
- Venture into the forest where you will engage in an interactive and personal journey
- Interact with many people to learn about the castles and villages, knights and wizards
- Create good relationships as you move from trusted contact

to trusted contact, learning more and more about the market and where you can locate castles that would be likely to welcome you

- Use a core message to help your contacts to help you find what you are looking for in your search

You engage in rapid relationship and trust building and develop your virtual Round Table.

On your journey, you will have a helpful companion, namely, your trusty laptop computer. Your laptop is your research buddy to help you learn more about the realm you are trying to connect with (industry/ field) and the people you are trying to find in the forest who are connected to the realm you want to join.

You will be putting together a *master list* of people who are doing the work you want to do and workplaces that your research indicates could be likely prospects to target for your quest. You grow and refine your list as your search moves forward and you learn more from the knights and wizards you meet with.

When you find helpful people you can ask them to join your virtual Round Table to provide you guidance as you continue your search.

In every heroic quest there are characters with whom the hero meets and interacts.

Some are helpful and others are not. This quest is no different.

Although you will begin by talking with your own close circle of friends and colleagues, you will soon talk with people who are friends and colleagues of your initial group but who are complete strangers to you. That process of talking with strangers can be pretty daunting. You do not know how they will respond to you until you try to communicate with them. You risk being embarrassed or disappointed by them, especially if you have been let go or if you have been looking for work for a long time. You are likely nervous about how these strangers might react if they hear about that. You might feel uncertain about what to say because you have not done this sort of networking before. You will learn how to handle those situations as we proceed.

Your job on this quest is to seek out people who are natural counselors who will meet with you and help you to find your way: these are your **knights** and **wizards**. They are crucial for the success of your quest.

Knights are people who are already employed in the industry or field in which you are trying to find work.

Wizards (usually forty to seventy years old) have been living a long time in the work realm you are trying to join. They are so well-positioned and central to the castles and villages and so knowledgeable about the community you are trying to join that, if they are willing to help you, they can cut down your search time significantly.

It is important to know how to engage and talk with knights and wizards. Some of them will be so helpful to you that they will join your *virtual round table* – your advisors, business associates, and personal friends who will help you during your quest and long after your job search is over. You will learn more about the knights and wizards as we proceed.

Much of your quest will take place in the forest.

You will find your way through the woods as you locate and meet the natural counselors in the realm you want to join, find out about places that could work well for you, learn how to approach a particular castle, and learn about places that are busy, active, growing, and have a good reputation.

You can meet knights and wizards in many settings.

They might be at a conference you attend or you might learn about a knight or a wizard from another wizard – perhaps your current or former professor – or you might consciously seek out a particular knight or wizard because you have heard this person will help you and is living in the village behind the castle and knows the castle staff.

One of the most effective ways to interact quickly with the community you seek to become part of is to join associations and participate immediately in group activities. If you can get involved with the committees representing your target neighborhood and take an active role, that engagement can create immediate potential to learn more information and meet more people. For example, volunteer to organize the next panel discussion or conference or write a report for a committee.

Your activity in a professional association will also enhance your ability to offer gifts of promotion and connection to the knights and wizards you will meet on your quest, which matters when you are trying to be helpful to others in the realm and do good deeds to assist other people professionally.

As you go down the paths in the forest looking for helpful people who will tell you about the community or marketplace (the specific industry and group of workplaces connected to that industry) you seek and the castles in that community, you will also encounter people who will not help you.

These are **ogres**. Think of them as your personal Darth Vader from Star Wars or the Wicked Witch of the West

34

from the Wizard of Oz. It is important that you not lose heart if you encounter an ogre who discourages you or discredits your efforts in some way.

Part of the challenge of any quest is to stay undaunted in the face of difficulties that arise as you seek your goal. The good news is that there are many more knights and wizards than there are ogres in the forest. You will learn more about ogres in this book and how to deal with them, including the possibility that you could be an ogre to yourself.

You get comfortable with starter conversations and learn that more magic happens in person.

The best way to advance your quest is to interact with the people in the forest and the villages. You will have many *starter conversations* that you use to gauge whether the contact person you have met is a wizard or an ogre. You will be able to tell this within the first few minutes of your conversation using the *voice test*, which you will learn more about as we proceed.

When you find knights or wizards in the forest, you want to try to meet with them in person for breakfast, lunch, dinner, or coffee because *more magic happens in person.*

When you meet with each contact, you should:

- Try to gain information through long, gossipy, rumor-filled conversations about what is happening in those realms (the professional communities /industries) you are trying to join that may be known to this contact.
- Try to learn about the castles you are interested in knowing more about.
- Elicit information on more knights and wizards who live in those villages or areas surrounding the castles.

- Show your *master list of people and places* to the knights and wizards and ask them to help you meet more knights and wizards in the realms where you are trying to connect.

In this meeting use your Core Message instead of talking about where to find jobs in this field.

In short, you want to tell the knights and wizards your *core message, which includes*:

1. Your *dream and dilemma*
2. A clear description or *prototype* of the type of job you seek
3. *Master lists of people and places* that will help the knights and wizards give you good advice, information, and market knowledge, which puts them in the role of being your career counselors/market advisors but not your recruiter (you are not asking them to help you locate jobs)

The way you message and advocate in these meetings matters a lot, so we will learn about that as we proceed.

You also want to do **good deeds.**

Many job seekers think the job search is only about getting a job. The outstanding networkers are giving back to people whether they are directly helped or not.

This quest is not just about you getting your job, it's also about you adding value to the realm you want to join and supporting those who advance your quest. You are creating trust relationships in the community you want to join and be a part of for the rest of your career. You are also developing a team that supports and advises you in your job search, and you want to support and help them in return. Think of this team as your own personal *knights and wizards of a virtual round table.* You will read about the process of creating trust relationships as we proceed.

You can learn a lot from the knights and the wizards that you meet on your journey about finding the right castles if you message well and know how to conduct a productive in-person meeting.

You master the formula for getting hired.

Throughout your quest, you will be looking for the castles that fit a four-part *Formula for Getting Hired* that consists of:

1. **Matching your skill set** to the needs of the workplace

2. Assessing **workflow**
3. Learning about the backgrounds of others already at the workplace to see if your background is likely to match the **culture** of the workplace
4. **Working on coming to the attention of the workplace through a trusted contact,** ideally with an endorsement

The first three elements can be discovered through research, but the fourth element requires meeting with a lot of people, which is the reason you need to get into the woods and have a lot of conversations and positive interactions with key people.

There are some overarching concepts to employ as you work your quest:

+ *More magic happens in person*
+ *Trust transfers*
+ *Open the treasure chests with your dream and dilemma*
+ *Opportunism creates more good luck*

We will learn about these overarching concepts that you can use to move your search forward.

Through this search process, you will find places that might work for you that also have enough work to be motivated to hire. You can use the *Formula for Getting Hired* as an assessment tool to help you determine if you are at this juncture.

You learn when to move into Campaign to Be Hired mode.

When you know that your skill set matches, the workplace has good workflow, your background is comparable to others who are already working there, and you can come to the attention of the workplace through a trusted contact, you have reached the *tipping point* in your quest.

Once you know where you want a job and which workplaces would be likely to welcome you, at that tipping point, you shift into a *Campaign to Be Hired* mode. You now want to look for the path that leads to the back of those castles. Behind every castle is a vibrant village full of people who know the castle staff and have the power to introduce you to them. A larger castle is far more accessible when you come in the side door or back door even if you must send your résumé to the front drawbridge where the dragon is stationed.

You want to do your best to be opportunistic, finding a way to meet with the knights or wizards connected with the castles you have targeted in your quest. You use creativity, humor, and intuitive judgment to find people and you always help and support others in the process.

Your goal is to go through a trusted contact to gain the attention of the key keeper, staying mindful that you do not want to be a pest or overly aggressive in your efforts. It is important to assess the strength of an endorsement you are likely to get from this knight or wizard. Is it likely to be weak or strong? Can you strengthen it by meeting in person and being generous and helpful? Intuitive judgment is important in this campaign.

You learn the importance of the right kind of endorsements.

Since endorsements can be strong or weak, it is important to understand the difference. A strong endorsement is one where the person knows you, likes you, knows your work and work ethic, knows someone inside the castle who has a position of influence and is also willing to say good things about you. Part of the challenge of the quest is to find people connected with the castle, meet up with them in person if possible, create trust and friendship, and find out if they will vouch for you.

Online endorsements have become popular on LinkedIn, but these may not be the kinds of endorsements that will open castle doors unless a stronger connection has already been made or can be developed by meeting in person or by using Skype to interact in a more personal and engaged way. It can be helpful to have someone suggest that based on your skill set alone you could be a good fit for a certain company, but far more helpful if the person gets to meet you, shake hands, and interact.

You learn that any meeting can be an informal interview.

That meeting is really an **informal interview** and an opportunity to create greater trust. That in-person connection will usually generate a more robust endorsement if you make a good impression and have the right skills and attitudes for the workplace. The endorsement will also be more robust if the endorser has seen you in action in a professional or other setting that helps to create a positive image. A client of mine who played recreational hockey on a men's team with other guys in his field not only found a good job prospect through that group but was endorsed by the people on his team who knew a lot about him from the way he played the game. You can also gain endorsements from people who meet you through volunteer activities, internships, workshops and many other recreational activities including religious groups and affinity groups.

If you conduct your quest the right way from the start of your adventure, you will be meeting people for breakfast, lunch, dinner and coffee, or in their offices. These meetings are called different things: informational interviews, informal meetings, formal interviews, or just lunch.

Whatever that meeting is called, it could lead to a job. You want to be comfortable with your Core Message and be ready to have a good discussion. If you have a good discussion, you are essentially having an informal *interview*, and if you have a good interview, you are more likely to land a job. We will talk about interviews and how to get ready to have them.

In short, your overarching goal is rapid relationship and trust building in the realm where you want to live for the rest of your career.

The goal of the quest is to find your way to meet with the key keeper by getting an introduction from the knights and wizards connected to the castle.

It is especially effective if you can come to the attention of the workplace through a trusted contact where the workplace has a need for someone with your background, there is work there that you are trained to do, and you have endorsements from people known to the castle staff.

It is even more promising, but not essential, if you are the only job seeker knocking at the castle's back or side door.

Even if the workplace has no current need, the castle may have a future need. Once you have created a positive connection there, your chances for being considered for a future job are enhanced.

This, in short, is the blueprint for a productive job search.

Done the right way, your quest is invaluable for both your current job search and your entire career.

+ Searching for a job by creating trust relationships in the realm where you want to live for your whole career allows you to create business friendships that sustain you throughout your career.

- These are the people who will be there for you if you ever need to find another job.
- These are the people who provide the basis for future business development.
- In a world where job security is swiftly becoming a thing of the past, many of us will need to find new opportunities and job prospects over and over again in our careers. We all need strong networks to keep our careers afloat and a blueprint for job search that helps us know how to create new prospects effectively.

None of the effort you put into this quest is wasted time.

Success in your quest will depend on such things as your ability to:

- Learn where the work is
- Figure out where you fit into the market
- Be creative about how to meet with the knights and the wizards
- Be assertive but not aggressive, bold but not obnoxious, persistent but not a pest
- Learn about the castles and surrounding villages
- Learn how to talk with the knights and wizards
- Help them do a better job of helping you advance your search
- Create a positive buzz about yourself in the neighborhood where you want to work by being a good person
- Have fun in the process

These are the key concepts of your job quest.

There are some additional activities in the back of this book that will help you prepare for the quest. If you use them, you will be more focused and proceed more quickly.

Now let's talk about how to prepare.

Part II

Preparation

Where you figure out your career sweet spot, are ready with your core message, know and use the formula for landing jobs, and create a basket of skills version of your résumé.

Chapter Five: How to Prepare for Your Quest

You want to be packed and ready for the journey. These steps will provide you with important information and knowledge about yourself and the road ahead so you are ready to help others guide you in your search for the right job.

THERE ARE FOUR ITEMS to prepare and take with you on your job quest. There is also one thing you may need to leave behind.

WHAT TO PACK:

One: Figure out Your Career Sweet Spot

1. What are your career AIMS?
2. What AILS you? (or could in the future)
3. What are the essential elements for your career?
4. What is the right career match for you?

Two: Be Ready with Your Core Message

1. Articulate your dream and dilemma
2. Clearly describe what you seek
3. Create a master list of people and a master list of places
4. Grow the master lists

Three: Know and Use the Formula for Getting Hired

1. Your skill set matches
2. The workplace has good workflow

3. The culture is a good match
4. You come to the attention of the workplace through a trusted contact

Four: Create a Basket of Skills Version of Your Résumé

WHAT TO UNPACK:

1. Emotional baggage

You would not go on a trip without packing your bag. You would not go hiking without boots and a map or GPS system to guide you. You would not set off on a sailboat without knowing how to work the sails. Preparation for a journey can make all the difference in the success of the venture. You are the hero of this quest, and it is up to you to conquer challenges and find your way to the castles that will fulfill your mission. It is important to perform this five-step preparation, because it will provide you with information and knowledge about yourself and the road ahead so you can help yourself and help others guide you in your search for the right job.

One: Figure out Your Career Sweet Spot

1. What Are Your Career AIMS?

How do you know the right career path to take? There are four elements that can help you to figure this out. These elements create the acronym AIMS. If you can identify these four elements, they will provide you with guidance so you can start your job search in the right direction. The four elements are Aptitudes, Interests, Market Need, and Skills. Assessment materials that can help you figure this out are available in the Appendices at the back of this book and as a download from my website: http://www.nielsencareerconsulting.com/jobquest/.

Aptitudes

What comes easily to you? What are your natural talents? Aptitudes are sometimes referred to as "gifts." Are you good at working with numbers? Do you understand people well? Are you always chosen as the leader in a group? Aptitudes are usually identifiable by your friends, your family, and your teachers. Make a list of your natural talents.

Interests

Interests and aptitudes are not always perfectly aligned. But if you have an interest in something that you also have an aptitude for, it can help when you are defining a good career direction. For example, you are visual by nature. You remember vivid scenes from the past. You love to arrange things like the furniture in your family home or your bedroom. You are very interested in shows about designing the interiors of homes. You received excellent marks in school for the way you organized projects. These aptitudes and interests may point to home design or real estate development or staging as well as other possibilities linking these talents and interests. Identify your strong interests and link them to careers where those interests and talents will be valuable and well utilized. If you are interested in the concepts, the thoughts, and the activities in which you would engage in this career, your chances of maintaining interest on a long-term basis will be greater.

Market Need

There has to be sufficient work in a particular field or industry for a career to be viable and stable. You might be talented and have a strong interest in something where there are so few jobs that the chances for opportunities are limited. Even if you find a job in the field, getting another good job in the field could be difficult unless you are a total standout. Megyn Kelly is a news anchor on Fox News who transitioned from a career in the law. She took a gamble when she made that transition, but her talent for being an on air personality was so evident, that she received multiple offers early in her bid to become a broadcast journalist. Not everyone could make that happen, especially in a tight, competitive market. To assess market need, check out the number of postings online, read trade journals, talk with professionals in the industry, and look for industry projections for jobs online in articles and in federal reports. In general, you would like to search for work in a hungry market to achieve greater career options and stability.

Skills

Some books and magazine articles tell the job seeker to "Do what you love and the rest will follow." It might be tempting to think that way, but

I have seen the harsh reality of trying to land a job without the requisite hard skills. Even if your skills transfer well or translate reasonably well, it can be difficult to convince an employer to take a chance on you. Certainly if you are an entrepreneur, then you do not face the same impediments to being hired. You are your own boss! However, not everyone is cut out to be a successful entrepreneur.

There is also a far less rigorous vetting process when family and friends are the people in charge of hiring. Many of my clients who want to transition to a new field find their jobs through the portal of businesses or ventures run by family and friends who know and trust them already or want to groom them to eventually take over the business. Missing skills can be gained over time by taking classes or learning on the job, but most employers will require a hard skill set that matches the needs of the workplace already. This is particularly true in a tight market.

When assessing the right career direction, you want to know what is going to work well for you. Assess your own personal talents, interests, and skills to figure that out.

2. What AILS You? (Or Could)

How do you know whether you will be happy in a particular career or job? What four elements can help you predict your job satisfaction? *Aptitude, Interest, Lifestyle,* and *Self-Actualization.* These elements create the acronym *AILS.* They can help you figure out *what AILS you.* If you have these four elements in your work-life, it is highly likely that you will enjoy your career and be relatively happy going to work. If your current job is not satisfying, or if sometime in the future you feel dissatisfied with your job or career, this exercise will help identify the source of your dissatisfaction.

The AILS acronym resulted from working with many unhappy professionals and helping them to understand what was wrong and what needed to change to make their careers more satisfying. But you do not have to wait until you are unhappy in your career to use this assessment tool to quickly figure out problems you could have if you launch your career in a direction that is potentially wrong for you. Think through your aptitudes and interests, the lifestyle you want, and the culture you need in a workplace before you launch your career/job quest so that you can ask the hard questions you need to ask in order to learn if the field will be right for you when you talk with people in the industry. No job or career will be perfect, but if you can get a close enough match based on your uniquely personal needs, you will be more satisfied in the long run. Assessment materials that can help you figure this out are available in the Appendices at the back of this book and as a download from my website: http://www.nielsencareerconsulting.com/jobquest/.

Aptitudes

How well do you understand the work you need to do for the job? If the work is easy for you, generally speaking, and you understand what you need to learn and can learn it quickly, you probably have an aptitude for this work. How do you know if you have an aptitude? Where others might struggle for comprehension, you already get it or can learn it quickly. When you studied this subject in school, you did well with reasonable effort. Colleagues, professors, or supervisors tell you that you are a quick study. If you do not know what your aptitudes are, there are testing services that can help you identify them.

Interests

Interests and aptitudes are not the same. You can be very interested in a subject but lack the aptitude. You can have an aptitude but lack interest in the subject. Many people who do not enjoy their careers report a lack of interest the content or subject matter. Given a wide array of books or magazines to read, they would not even choose to read about matters related to the industry they are in. If you lack interest in the work you do, the content of your daily work is likely to be boring for you. Ultimately that lack of interest makes it hard to continue to do an outstanding job. For example, if you are in IT but bored by programming and you really enjoy interacting with people, you might want to plan a move into the role of the business systems analyst, for example, or another role in the field where you can have greater personal interaction.

Another issue that arises around the concept of interest has to do with a strong interest or passion for a career or job that is not reasonably achievable because of other priorities. For example, you would love to be a film critic or write the next great thriller series, but you have a young family, and you want to keep making a lot of money as a financial analyst. You can try to build in elements of the kind of work you love as a hobby or do some of what you love during your leisure time. You might be able to write a blog or write a column for a professional magazine. If you have other unmet strong interests in helping others, you might try to engage in community service, volunteer work, or other activities that satisfy that need to some extent. Eventually, you may be able to transition your career in a direction that includes more of your passions or strong interests, depending on what they are and your particular situation. There can often be a second life for your career as your priorities shift over time.

Second Careers

Many professionals find a way to develop a second career over time while relying on their primary careers to fund that venture. Some people create second careers by gaining credentials in new fields, while others create businesses that can allow a leap into a totally new field. For example, a lawyer with a passion for designing wedding dresses continued to work as a lawyer, while her sister created a wedding gown business in New York. It was gratifying for her to be able to fund the business and be involved in its evolution. She may eventually transition her career to work there full time and leave the law altogether. Another former partner at a large law firm developed a series of weight loss clinics while he continued to work in his primary field. He built up the business for a number of years, eventually leaving his six figure job once the clinics were doing well enough to provide him with a good income. Another person transitioned to a career in interior decorating by helping her husband's business furnish and decorate corporate offices. That experience allowed her to move into a totally new field without the re-credentialing usually needed for interior decorating. Another professional transitioned to a full time job in alumni relations by engaging in extensive volunteer work for his alma mater's local alumni chapter. Other people have created second careers by going back to school, retooling their skill set to become psychologists, teachers, nurses, archivists, librarians, and much more. Unless friends and family open the door to a radically new career, many people will need to go back to school or take classes to gain new skills in a certification program. An exception to that general rule can sometimes occur if the new career is one that serves the primary field or makes use of knowledge or relationships gained in the primary industry even though the person no longer functions in that field, per se. To use the field of law as an example, JD preferred careers include: legal recruiter; law school administration, including career services for a law school; marketer for a law firm; professional development in a law firm; consulting to the legal industry, including e-discovery roles, such as project manager and consultant; journalist for a legal magazine; director of legislative affairs for a company; lobbying; global information communication roles; trust officer at a bank; compliance positions; financial planner; and director of communications for a company or not-for-profit, to name a few. Careers related to the primary field can serve as a training ground for a new career direction, allowing the professional to skirt formal education that would normally be required to qualify for the new career. Once in the new field, it can be useful to gain knowledge by taking courses or certification programs in the new industry. The on ramps vary depending on the industry. A good way to find the on ramps is by doing informational interviews with people who have made the transition and can tell you their story and refer you to others who have transitioned and may have additional stories and insights.

Lifestyle

What kind of lifestyle do you need to be satisfied? Maybe your highest priority is to have a balance between your work and your home life. Maybe you need to be sure you can leave your stresses and worries at work and not take them home with you. Perhaps you believe you need to make six figures to feel secure. Perhaps you need to make enough money to support a growing family and allow your spouse to be home with the children. These and other elements influence your lifestyle satisfaction level.

Self-Actualization

What kind of person do you want to be? The culture of your workplace and the type of work you do has an impact on you. How you respond to the people you interact with at work, your clients, the work you do, the pace of your work, and your colleagues' attitudes all interact with your unique personality to shape the person you are and are becoming. If you work in a pressure-cooker environment that makes you feel extremely irritable and you bring that attitude home with you, creating tension in your family, your workplace environment may be having a negative impact on your life. Your behavior is being shaped in a way that is likely to create a negative response in people around you both in and out of the workplace. You might attempt to combat it by ignoring what is happening at work. But it is not easy for most people to change their natural responses to their work environments. The same intense workplace culture that makes you crazy could be a great environment for someone who thrives on being in a hectic or fast-paced setting. That person might enjoy the beehive-of-activity aspect of the workplace and not experience it as overly stressful. Every person's path to self-actualization is unique.

How is the workplace culture affecting you? Do you like the person you are and are becoming? Or do you go through your day feeling drained, bored, angry, annoyed, or anxious? Are you bringing your stresses home with you? Are you spending so much time by yourself in front of your computer doing research that you are feeling disconnected and depressed? Do you need a more social, team-oriented workplace? If you are required to work fast under pressure, are you finding that to be a challenge that adds to your sharpness or are you feeling overwhelmed? If you have to be decisive to excel on the job, is that making you tougher or are you becoming bitter? Does the work you do or your workplace culture require that you compromise your ethics or honesty?

The work we choose to do and the place we choose to work have the power to shape our personalities. You want to be sure you like the result you are getting. If you don't, you may need to find a different environment or, in some cases, a different career. What works well for one person does not always work well for another, so solutions vary: changing something, such as moving to a new team or department can sometimes solve the problem. Sometimes more radical steps need to be taken, such as changing your career altogether.

Finding a Better Fit for Your Personality

A number of years ago, I worked with an energetic, hard-working associate with an engaging personality who began her career in labor and employment law. After years of courtroom battles, however, she had become a tough-minded, abrasive litigator, which helped her succeed in her job but caused problems in her life. She brought that attacking attitude home with her, and not only had sleepless nights and headaches, but also fought with her husband over "every little thing." They divorced. About a year later, she met a wonderful man and they decided to get married. She came to me for career counseling because she was worried that she would ruin her second marriage if she continued to practice law as a litigator. Being a litigator brought out her inner warrior, but she did not like the effect on her personality or the toll on her health or relationships. After considering alternatives, she decided to move into the field of human resources as an HR coordinator for a midsize company and was able to make that transition doing an effective networking search. This transition permitted her to soften her personality and relax into the role of a more collegial team member. She was even more successful in this career than she had been as a litigator because the setting allowed her to use her personal strengths and natural sociability.

3. What Are the Essential Elements for Your Career?

What do you need to be successful in your work life? For a job to be satisfying on a long-term basis, you want to be sure the workplace satisfies your personal needs. If you are unhappy with your job, you are more likely to leave or be fired. This is not good for your career or your self-esteem. You want to have a job that plays to your strengths as a person as well as contributes to your professional skills. If you know what you are looking for, you can vet the workplace for your needs, but to do this, you need to be knowledgeable about yourself. Assessment materials that can help you figure this out are available in the Appendices at the back of this book and as a download from my website: http://www. nielsencareerconsulting.com/jobquest/.

The Essential Elements exercise helps you identify which elements you need in your career and your work life to create satisfaction and which irritants to avoid. This exercise helps you create your unique template for a satisfying work life and find the matches for that in the field of potential workplaces.

Start with your work history. For this exercise, you'll assess what you liked and did not like about each of your past jobs. This is the key to spotting trends that should affect your choice of future workplaces and/ or careers.

To do your work history, write down every job you have had, paid or unpaid, including volunteer work. Then create a plus and a minus column for each job and list everything you liked or disliked about each position. Include college and professional school as well. When you have finished this list, look at it to see if you can find recurring themes and trends. You can ask friends and family to help you with this assessment if you need assistance to spot the trends. A trend might be that you always seem to like a job if you like the people you are working with and the content of the work doesn't really matter to you very much. Or you need to feel your work has a mission you really care about and that motivates you. Or you hate jobs when you have to work under stress or when you feel bored or have a micromanager boss. Everyone has a unique profile that emerges from this exercise, but the trends will appear if you look for them. These trends usually reveal consistent and powerful needs that you have to meet to have a satisfying work life. From these trends you can create two lists: one is a list of your "Essential Elements" and the other is your "Irritants to Avoid."

Write down the roles you want to have as part of your work life on your list of Essential Elements. Do you require an uptick on the learning curve to stay engaged? Put *mental variety* on the list. Do you need stability and security? Put *stability/security* on the list. How much money do you need to make to pay your debts and feel secure? Be sure to add that to your list of essential elements.

Next, create a second list of all the elements you can find from your work history that make you annoyed, irritated, angry, or feel some other negative experience that you would like to avoid. Does a micromanaging boss or lack of control over your hours make you very annoyed? What pushes your buttons? Do you need an office instead of a cubicle so that you can concentrate and stay focused? Try to identify only those irritants that make you feel truly "allergic" or repulsed. These go on your Irritants to Avoid list.

After you have your two lists, create a scale next to each element. The scale should range from 1 to 10. The Essential Elements Appendix has an illustration that was created from a work history. Next, give every element you have identified a rank on a scale of 1 to 10, with 10 the most positive rating. Each element gets a separate rating. You are rating how much you want to have this element in your work life. If you give something on your list a 9 or 10, that means you really should not take a job if it does not provide that element. If you give an element only a 5 or lower, you should consider taking it off of your list because it is not essential enough to make a difference in your choice of a particular job or career.

When it comes to ranking the list of elements you want to avoid, you are measuring how much you hate that element. If you give something a 10, you would not want to take a job that would require that you put up with that element in your daily work life. For example, if you do not work well under pressure and you hate pressure so much you give it a rating of 10, then you should try to avoid jobs that require that you deal with intense pressure on a daily basis. If, however, you dislike pressure but you give it a 6, that would indicate that you could manage some pressure even if you do not like it. You would look for jobs where you only have to cope with moderate pressure on a daily basis.

Once you have two lists of elements reflecting what you need to have and to avoid in your work life and you have ranked each element, you have a template of your work life requirements. You can use this template to measure or vet a potential job or a career for your unique needs. As you learn more about a workplace or a career over the course of your quest, you will be able to make reasonably accurate guesses about how well that particular workplace/career is likely to match your needs. The template also helps guide you during your quest in asking questions that will give you the information you need to assess whether the job you are considering will be a good match for you. For example, if a "screamer" boss is on your list of irritants, you want to discreetly ask questions as you network with people loosely affiliated with a given workplace to learn how the manager you would be working with behaves under pressure. Discovering a "screamer" should be a factor in your decision to work there or to keep looking for a workplace that might be a better fit for you.

The template you create can change over time, so it is a good idea to update your template over the course of your career. A change in priorities can occur in your life that will affect the essential elements or irritants you feel most strongly about. For example, if you have a baby, the need to have predictable time to be with your child or the need for greater balance between work and home life might suddenly pop to a 10 on your Essential Elements list. The irritant of being unable to control your hours might jump to a 10. This change in priority would affect your job satisfaction and your need to make a career or job change. Another example of a shift in priorities that can occur happens later in careers when people think about retirement or semi-retirement. Another shift can happen when a parent or loved one is in need of help; this can create a time commitment that affects the amount of time you have available for work.

Once you create your template, you can apply it to your current job to learn what is satisfying and is not satisfying for you when it comes to your present work life. You are essentially vetting your workplace for your needs. For example, if you currently have a job that does not allow you a chance to have variety and you assign a 9 to that element but you are getting a 2 from the current job, then the job is flunking when it comes to that important need. You can get along for a while with a serious mismatch such as that, but over time it will take its toll. If you are missing out on many of your deeply felt needs, you may want to launch a job quest to find a job that is a better fit for you.

Two: Be Ready with Your Core Message

1. Articulate Your Dream and Dilemma

As you talk with people, it is important to help your contacts help you. The people you meet who are willing to assist you often do not know how to do that effectively. It is your job to instruct them and guide them so they can provide the information you need. How do you do that?

Tell your contacts *your dream* and *your dilemma*. You can also use the words *goal* and *problem*, or *objective* and *difficulty*. If you can clearly define your goal and your problem for your contacts, they will have an easier time knowing how to help you.

How can you identify your dream, objective, or goal? Use your Essential Elements analysis to identify positions and fields that you think could be a good match for you. If you have trouble doing this, then you need to talk with people in the field doing the work you think you might want to do to see if their experiences support your educated guesses about what it would be like to work in their job. By talking with people who already do the work you think you want to do and using the template you create from your Essential Elements exercise, you will be able to find good matches.

Articulating your dilemma or problem is important. You need help to solve your problem, and the contact person is in a position to be helpful to you by providing information.

> "I am having trouble finding people who do event planning for corporations, because I just don't travel in those circles even though I have skills in event planning. Can you think of good organizations to join? Can you think of good trade journals or blogs or websites to go to so I can read more? Can you think of nice people you know doing the kind of work I want to do?"

> "I am having difficulty finding out about these smaller companies and firms because they are not large enough to be written about in trade journals. I need to talk with people who know something about this small company market because they work in a small company themselves. I could use help finding these people. Do you know anyone nice who is doing this kind of work who would take the time to teach me more about this business community?"

Once you have done that, you can create an image or a *prototype* for the kind of job that you would like to have.

2. Clearly Describe What You Seek

What is a prototype? Your goal is to find a job, but not just any job. You want to be specific and clear. You should create prototypes or illustrations that are reminiscent of an ad that clearly define the type of position you think would be a good fit for your skills and background and the type of work that exists in the market. Here are some examples:

> "I am looking for a position with a small respected litigation boutique that is busy, active, and growing, where people like to work. So I am searching for places that fit that description, even if they are not currently advertising. Do you know of places that fit that description? And if you do, do you know of any nice, helpful, friendly people who work there who might talk with me so I can learn more about that workplace and others that are similar?"

The key word is "nice." Everyone knows who is nice, friendly, and helpful and who is not. If you find the nice people in the world, you are finding the knights and the wizards who will help you learn more.

> "I am looking for midsize companies that are busy and growing and that have programmers already working there."

> "Do you know of real estate agents who know about staging or might use stagers and who are nice people that I could contact so I could learn more about this field?"

The prototype you provide helps your contacts identify the right group of places to consider and talk about with you. If the prototype is overly specific, however, the contact person might have trouble identifying many possible places that fit the description. You want to create an ad that is specific enough to prompt your contact to identify workplace possibilities but not so specific that you eliminate too many options.

3. Create a Master List of People and Places

Your job quest will advance if you talk in-depth with many contacts. You want to develop a *master list of people and places* – people you would like to meet who are doing the work you would like to be doing, and places that you want to know more about. You grow these lists as your search progresses. Throughout your search, you should show these two lists to anyone you know even tangentially connected with the realm or village you are trying to join. It is important to learn something about the castles that could be a good fit for you, and the knights and wizards who work there. Ask your contacts, "Do you know any of these people, and if so, are they *helpful people* or *nice guys*? What, if anything, do you know about these workplaces?" Even if your contacts may not be associated with the castle you're interested in, it doesn't hurt to share the list. You may discover that your contact knows a knight, wizard, or other castle personnel through other associations. Sample master lists are available in the Appendices at the back of this book and as a download from my website: http://www.nielsencareerconsulting.com/jobquest/.

One of my clients was fired by his law firm only one year into his career at the tail end of the recent recession. This could have been a career-ending event, but he employed the approach in this book. He landed the job he targeted at a more prestigious firm in New York and will make more money than he was making at his previous job. In addition, his job search opened up two more opportunities he could have landed had he wanted to pursue them. When I asked him to explain how he had conducted his search so quickly, he said it was the result of the ideas he had gotten from our training session about rapid relationship and trust building. He was able to quickly expand his close connections in ways that surprised him. "I learned that I had connections I had no idea I had." And one of them bore fruit. One of the wizards he had coffee with in his quest turned out to be one of the partners on the interviewing team at the firm where he was hired. Expect the unexpected when it comes to this kind of relational job quest. Clients routinely discover connections they had no idea they had and build connections they had no idea they could build.

One of my clients was a new law school graduate with enhanced knowledge in the health care field. She had a certificate in health care from her law school, won an award for excellence in health law regulation, wrote for the school's health law journal, and was a board member of the Health Law Institute. She read an article in the legal newspaper about two of the smaller local health law boutiques winning a ten-year contract to do work for the National Institutes of Health in an area of the law she had researched for one of her professors. She realized that she should try to maximize her networking efforts with respect to these two firms, even though neither firm seemed to be looking to hire anyone.

As part of her effort, she called the professor she had assisted, who had really liked her work for him on his project, and told him about her interest in these two firms. As luck would have it, he knew one of the partners at one of the firms named in the article and was happy to call his friend to put in a good word for her. She was able to land a job at this firm even though there was no job posted. Clearly, this search strategy based on market knowledge and proactive networking with one of the wizards from her round table increased her chances for that opportunity.

4. Grow the Master Lists

You have been learning about what is happening in your desired professional neighborhood and have some sense of where the work is flowing. You may have read a number of articles that report that some large castles are changing in certain ways and that new small companies have been created. Maybe you have read an article written by a consultant that reflects this trend and predicts more of the same. As a result, you make an educated guess that certain midsize companies might be willing to hire if they are trying to grow. You research the midsize companies that could be interested in you given your core competencies, using Google or other search engines. Next, you go to their websites and research the backgrounds of the people who work there. You discover that your background is similar to the backgrounds of other people who work at a number of these targeted companies. By doing this research, you are finding the castles where you might have a good fit and the knights and wizards you would like to talk with. You might also see postings for positions requiring your skill set, which is often a good sign. This castle needs help and is actively hiring. Even if the workplace has a dragon or two at the gate, the castle staff might welcome your inquiry, especially if you come to their attention through a trusted contact, ideally with a strong endorsement. This is useful information for your quest. As you learn of good prospects this way, be sure to add them to your master lists.

Which people go on your master list?
+ People doing the work you think you want to do
+ People in the neighborhood you are trying to join
+ People connected to the castles you are trying to vet

What places go on your master list?
+ Places that could be a good fit for your skill set and background
+ Places you learn about that are rumored to be busy and may be growing
+ Places that your research indicates could be getting more work soon
+ Places where your skill set could transfer and be valuable

Start with what you learn from your research. Even after you embark on your job quest, you will continue to uncover more information about the people and places in the neighborhoods you seek to join. Magazine or Internet articles from a wide variety of sources can be very helpful as you try to learn about the people and places that could be good matches for you. Trade journals can be useful also. Social networking sites such as LinkedIn can be used to assist your search for specific people in the right neighborhoods. Using Google or other search engines to find the backgrounds of the people who are important for your search can be one of the easiest ways to learn about people and places to add to your master list.

The master lists of people and places are important for your search because they will be a focal point for your networking discussions. Instead of talking about jobs, you want to talk about people and places: where the market is stronger, which places are busy and growing, and other information about what is happening in the neighborhood or realm you want to join.

Even if you do not mention the "J" word (talk immediately about jobs), the idea that you are looking for a job is obvious. You do not need to mention that you are looking for a job, because it is evident from your conversation. You are not putting your contact person on the spot by asking him or her to help you find a job or give you a job. If there is, in fact, a need for someone with your background at the castle where this contact is connected and if you have made a good impression and created trust, this contact person will be quietly vetting you for a job even without being directly asked by you to do so. As we shall see in Chapter Eleven: The Tipping Point and the Campaign Phase, there is also a way for you to raise the idea of a job possibility with your wizard or knight once you are at the "tipping point" by using certain magic words.

Before you launch your quest, be prepared to discuss your dream/ dilemma or goal/problem. When you articulate your goal and problem, the people you meet will be far more helpful to you. Be ready to create an image of the job or jobs you are looking for. And have at least a few names on your master list of people and places so you can grow that list with knights and wizards.

Three: Know and Use the Formula for Getting Hired

When job seekers I am working with come into my office and say four key things, I know it is highly probable that they will land a job. This is the **Formula for Getting Hired**:

1. Your *skill set matches* the needs of the workplace or is close enough to answer their need.
2. The workplace has good *workflow*.
3. The *culture is a good match*.
4. You have come to the attention of the workplace through a *trusted contact, ideally with an endorsement* if possible – especially one inside the castle or one who is good friends with the key keeper.

Use this formula for landing jobs to guide your search efforts. Try to make these four elements happen for you as you conduct your search. This calls for both research and relationship building.

Target castles that are likely to welcome you. As we have seen, that requires some Internet research to start, and then you can develop more knowledge in your conversations with natural counselors. You are looking for workplaces where:

1. Your Skill Set Matches

Your core competencies match their needs or your skill set is close enough that you can do the work with a fairly shallow learning curve.

You can often figure this out by talking with people who have worked at this castle in the recent past and by checking the website of the castle to learn the backgrounds of people currently working there. You can find them on LinkedIn, or use Google to look up their work history.

2. The Workplace Has Good Workflow

The workplace is growing and has work that needs to be done.

Finding the Deep Water

Our family went on a cruise to Alaska. When the ship docked at one of the towns near a river, there was an opportunity to take a rafting trip down the river. We signed up to go rafting along with many others from the cruise. When we arrived at the starting point, we were assigned to sturdy, inflated rafts that seated eight. The rafts had guides who told the passengers how and when to paddle and how to shift their weight to help the raft keep moving down the river. These directions were important at the time, because a recent drought meant that there was far less water flowing down this river than there had been in past summers. If we didn't work as a team and follow the guide's directions to keep the raft in the deeper water, it was likely to run aground.

As we started off, we quickly learned that the shallow water was everywhere and that the rocks and pebbles in the shallows would ground the boat. To get the boat moving again, everyone in the raft had to bounce up and down and urge the raft forward to get it off of the shoals. Time and time again the rafts around us ran aground, and we saw the passengers bumping up and down to urge their rafts off of the rocks and pebbles. Our guide was particularly good at keeping our raft in deep water. When I asked him how he did it, he told me that he had been guiding trips down this river for many years and that he knew where the water ran deeper. He had "studied up" on the river.

This is a good analogy for job search in a time of economic uncertainty. If there is a lot of shallow water out there, your job is to "study up" on where the work is flowing. You want to be informed about what is happening in the world generally, as well as locally. This keeps your career raft in deeper water.

You can figure this out by talking with knights and wizards to find out whether people at this workplace are busy. Are the people who work there talking about new work coming in? Are they complaining about how many hours they are working? Are they excited about a new client? Another source of workflow information can be found in articles in local online sources, blogs, and magazines. A manager who is interviewed for an article might reveal the company's plan to attract new business by using a different pricing structure or some innovation that will create more business.

3. The Culture Is a Good Match

Your personal background seems to be a good match for the workplace; you hit it off with people in that workplace in a formal or informal interview, or chance meeting. When compared with others who work there already, their backgrounds look like yours in terms of academic institutions, mutual friends, prior workplaces, comparable skills, experiences, and interests. If someone you know and like has joined this workplace and is satisfied, it is likely that the workplace culture will be good for you too. Once you find one or two people who work at a particular castle you think is a good match, you can learn about their backgrounds by using Google or LinkedIn. If you can locate at least one person who has recently worked there or knows someone who worked there, you can learn about his experiences by contacting him by e-mail or by phone, introducing yourself and asking if he would be willing to speak with you in confidence about his impressions of the workplace. This approach works best with people who are no longer affiliated with that castle and have less incentive to sugar coat their comments. It also works best if you have a friend or trusted contact who introduces you to the person who worked there in the past. And another source for this inside information can be the close friends and family of people who worked there in the past and know how that work situation was experienced by their friend or family member.

4. You Come to the Attention of the Workplace through a Trusted Contact

Finally, you come to the attention of the key people at the workplace through people they trust. This last element is the one that requires you to go on the quest because that is how you create trust relationships in the neighborhood you are trying to connect with or join. If you can come to the attention of the workplace through a mutually trusted contact, especially if that interaction can be in person and you are likeable and helpful to the people you encounter, your chance for landing a job there is greatly enhanced. Even if there is no current opening, when one develops, you are more likely to land it if you have come to the attention of the workplace and there is a positive buzz about you with the key keeper and other influential castle personnel. (Note: Recruiters with good relationships with castle staff also fit this description and can be *trusted contacts*, but remember that they also introduce the key keeper to the closest rival to you that they can find for the job.)

Four: Create a Basket of Skills Version of Your Résumé

If you are an employer looking for someone to help you, you want to find a person you could add to the team because he or she will fit in well, and who also has the core competencies needed to do the job. As a job seeker, you have to understand the skills and background you possess so that you can show the employer you have what it takes to do the job needed. Your résumé is your chance to tell the prospective employer your unique story. It is an advocacy piece. Your résumé is also a marketing piece that could convince the employer to meet with you for the all-important interview, whether it's formal or informal.

To create a good marketing piece, be sure your résumé conveys the following basic information to the prospective employer:

- The kind of job you want to have
- Your qualifications for that job
- Where you worked and who you worked for in the past
- Illustrations of success, especially doing comparable work

There are a number of excellent books and online articles on the topic of résumé writing, and there are a variety of résumé formats that you could use to convey your information.

Many people choose a chronological résumé style. That format shows relevant education, employment history, and experiences listed in chronological order starting with the most recent experience. The chronological résumé format highlights a consistent work history. If you have been working at one place for your entire career and you want to showcase your loyalty or show that you have worked your way up the ladder at one workplace, the chronological format can do that.

When it comes to rapid relationship and trust building, however, the chronological résumé has some drawbacks. Because it lists each job followed by a description of the work you did there, often the same or similar skill set is described again and again under each job listed. In a networking meeting, over lunch or coffee, you have very little time and a lot of ground you need to cover. You want the focus of the meeting to be your talk together. With a chronological résumé, the reader has to dig out the relevant skill set written under each job heading. A résumé can be cleaner and clearer if skills are listed just once at the top of the résumé. That "basket of skills" or skills-based format can provide an immediate, clear understanding of skills that you want the reader to see. You want your contact to think, "I like this person and – how lucky! – she has the skill set I am looking for or my friend with that new start-up could be looking for."

You can also choose to highlight the core competencies you want to emphasize based on the type of job you expect to learn about in your networking meeting. For example, if you have been working as an environmental lawyer on the litigation side, but you will be talking with an in-house counsel about compliance work in corporations in your informational meeting, you can highlight the skills you possess that are useful for compliance work at the top of your résumé. If your résumé highlights litigation skills, the person you are meeting with might not think you would be a good addition to her department, when you really could be a great match.

If you have worked as a programmer but you want a job as a business systems analyst and you already have had experience doing that job even if you did not yet have that title, you can highlight the skills that make you a good hire for the business systems analyst job at the top of your résumé. A sample basket of skills résumé template is available in the Appendices at the back of this book and as a download from my website: http://www.nielsencareerconsulting.com/jobquest/.

There is one last issue to be considered before you walk out the door, and that is your emotional readiness to undertake this adventure.

What to Unpack: Emotional Baggage

Before you set out on your journey, be sure you are not carrying excess emotional baggage that could weigh you down. Unpack those bags before you start your quest, if at all possible. Sometimes negative emotional baggage can stop you from ever getting out the door at all to conduct your job search. It takes energy to conduct an in-person job search. If you never get out the door, you will miss out on the most important aspect of the networking search, showing up in person, which is crucial for developing trust relationships. If you fail to manage strong negative emotions, those powerful feelings can interfere with and detract from your interview. Depression, anger, resentment, or other negative feelings can cause you to be seen by those you network with as bitter, sarcastic, or depressed, making you a poor choice for their workplace team.

At the start of the recession in 2009, I worked with an attorney who had been at her firm for three years. Anne had been let go by her firm after logging more hours than any of the other associates in her practice group the preceding year. She was considered to be a star performer by many of the partners in her group who entrusted their work to her. Anne had not even considered the possibility that she might lose her job until it happened to her. She thought her position with the firm was secure because so many partners relied on her, she was well-liked, and she was the top biller in her associate class. When she was laid off, I received a call from one of the partners who had worked closely with her. Since I was Anne's outplacement coach, the partner was calling to tell me what a wonderful lawyer and person this associate was, how much she had contributed to the practice group, and how much she would be missed by the partners she had worked with. She was the last associate they expected to be fired. The partner who called was also worried about Anne because she was so emotionally upset about being outplaced.

When I met with Anne it was obvious how upset she felt. Her eyes were bloodshot from bouts of crying. She was close to tears throughout our first conversation. She apologized for being so upset. She said she could not believe that this had happened to her. This was the first time in her life that she had failed at anything. She could not understand why the firm had let her go, because she had done everything right and worked extremely hard. She had given up much of her personal life to meet the expectations of her partners, and she had been told that she had been the standout associate in her class, most likely to succeed at the firm. We talked about the unfairness of this situation and how she was justified to be as upset as she was.

As we worked together in our sessions, it was clear to me that Anne was a bright, capable lawyer, just as her partner had described her to be. It was likely that she would land on her feet, but only if she could manage her emotions. Anne and I needed to address her emotional state. I encouraged her to talk about her feelings and passed her a box of tissues. After a few meetings, I suggested that her tears might be her way of expressing a pretty intense anger. That was an idea she could use. It was a turning point for her. After that she was able to divert the energy she had been putting into her sadness into more productive activities. For Anne, it was helpful to recognize that she was enraged about what happened to her and that her angry feelings were justified. After that she used her anger to motivate her search. No longer weepy, she felt more empowered and got to work finding a better job where she would be appreciated.

Anne had one of the fastest job searches I have ever witnessed. Her search lasted just over one month. She landed a good job at a litigation boutique. Part of her success was the result of her strong desire to do whatever she could to work hard on her search. Because she had been such a standout at her past firm, she had a group of enthusiastic partners who were ready and willing to assist her and endorse her when she asked for their help.

The key to overcoming destructive emotional baggage triggered by difficult circumstances, such as being fired, is to talk about your feelings with someone you trust. The person needs to be able to listen to you without telling you what you should feel or trying to get you to pretend you do not feel what you are experiencing. The person listening should not be judgmental.

How can you find such a person? Sometimes it is possible to find a job search partner who is struggling with the same or similar feelings.

If you attend a support group for professionals, you might meet someone you could pair up with for mutual support. Talking with a truly unbiased, supportive person can help you to recover your sense of equilibrium. Some people use meditation or mindfulness effectively to deal with difficult situations and clear their heads. For others, exercise can help. Still others might take up boxing or karate. There are many ways to let off steam and regain balance.

Most good therapists or counselors will be able to help you with this short-term goal as well. Professional counselors will support you and allow you to express difficult feelings. If, however, you experience a serious depression, which could include thoughts of suicide, plans to carry out a suicide, sleepless nights that do not abate, loss of appetite, or an inability to function during the day, it is important to seek help from a qualified mental health professional.

Turning to alcohol or drugs to get relief from bad feelings only masks the pain. It will not solve underlying emotional issues and can make your life a lot worse if your use becomes a habitual way of trying to cope.

It is important to learn to manage uncomfortable feelings, identify underlying emotions such as anger and helplessness, confront fears of humiliation or other fears, and deal with self-doubt. This is all part of the quest you are on. Often, it is our own personal sense of failure or humiliation that we ascribe to others that prevents us from conducting an effective interpersonal search. We assume other people think badly of us, when, in fact, we are our own harshest critics. And, for every person who does judge you harshly for getting fired or jumping from one job to another, there are more people who will understand, who have faced something similar, and who will support you. Part of the quest you are on is to find these people, to become friends, and to help them out, too. We are all vulnerable in our lives and we need to be there for each other.

Part III

Launch Your Quest

Where you learn how to find the key people to connect with, figure out how to get knights and wizards to meet with you and what happens when you do meet, learn the concept of friendship lite, find out what to do in interviews, and learn how to recognize the tipping point and move into the campaign phase.

Chapter Six: Finding the Key People to Connect With

You have done your preparation, and now you are ready to go out the door of your cottage, enter the forest, and look for knights and wizards who will help you find your way to the castles you think could be good for you.

WHAT YOU WILL DISCOVER when you enter the woods is that the forest is full of people who can and will help you. These are the knights and the wizards. You will also encounter a handful of people who will not be helpful. These are the ogres. You need to be ready to talk with the people you meet by:

+ Knowing how to find knights, wizards, and ogres
+ Using the starter conversation to find natural counselors
+ Using the voice test to sort out the knights and wizards from the ogres
+ Encouraging knights and wizards to meet with you in person

Who Are the Knights and Wizards?

Knights and wizards are the natural counselors of the world. They are people who enjoy helping, advising, and mentoring other people. They are engaged with and willing to assist others. Above all, they have figured out that what goes around comes around.

Knights and wizards are *nice people*. That may seem like an overly simplistic way to describe someone you are looking for, but it turns out to be the best way to find the right people to help you. Everyone knows who is nice and helpful and who is not. Asking "Who do you know at that workplace/committee/group who is a nice person?" or "Who do you know who might be kind enough to take the time to talk with me?" turns out to be one of the most effective ways to find the right people to look for on your journey.

Wizards and knights are similar in that they are both helpful to others; however, wizards have the distinction of being particularly well-positioned and knowledgeable about the castles and the villages surrounding them. They are especially valuable because they possess even greater information and power than some of the knights. The reason they have even more power to help you is that they are very well-connected in the community you are trying to join. Wizards tend to be more senior; they are usually around 40 to 70 years old. They have created many trust relationships in the realms they inhabit. They may have been college classmates with people who are now the managing partners at law firms or the CEOs or managers of businesses and they are well-positioned in their industry. They may go on fishing trips or ski trips with the gatekeepers and the key keepers in the professional community you are trying to connect with. They may have children in the same school or serve on boards with members of the castle staff. Even after people leave the workforce and retire, there

is still a period of time when they maintain connections into the vital center of a professional neighborhood.

Many new graduates hesitate to ask their parents or their parents' friends to help them with their job searches, but it is a mistake to exclude anyone who could be a wizard from assisting you with your quest.

Who Are the Ogres?

Ogres, on the other hand, are not going to help you, and sometimes they can interfere with your quest by damaging your motivation and attitudes about your job search. Do not be surprised when you meet ogres on your journey. Every adventure has to have a few challenges. Instead of retreating to the safety of your cottage, try to think about ogres differently so you can continue your quest.

The ogres of the world are people who generally avoid helping other people, not just you. Many of them are having a tough time in life. You might never learn why someone has become an ogre, but there could be important reasons for his or her behavior. Perhaps the person has cancer and has not told anyone yet. Maybe this person is painfully shy or never learned to relate well to other people. He may be in the middle of a crisis, such as a divorce, which is causing a lot of personal stress. You may never learn why a person has gone to the "dark side," but there could be an underlying reason. If you meet an ogre, the best approach is to try to be forgiving. Do not let an encounter with an ogre stop you from your quest. Keep looking for the knights and the wizards and have faith that you will find them. Even ogres know who the helpful, engaged people are in their neighborhood, so ask them if they can think of people who might be willing to spend time talking with you so that you can learn more about the industry.

It is also possible that someone who seems at first to be a knight or wizard could turn into an ogre during your conversation.

A good illustration of an encounter with an ogre who seemed at first to be a knight or wizard, comes from a woman I worked with a few years ago. Her story also illustrates the power of an ogre to damage a job seeker's attitude about conducting a job search.

Ginger graduated from a top-tier law school where she had done well academically. She found a job in a prestigious law firm after graduation. At first she enjoyed the work, but after a few years, she felt burned out and stressed out by the pace and demands of the job. She left the firm to take a break and do document review work, which allowed her a 9 to 5 work schedule with weekends off. After about a year of document review work, she felt ready to return to an associate position with a firm. Document review work was not satisfying for her. She wanted more of a challenge.

Associate positions are very different from document review and call for a higher level of skill. To be considered for an associate position on track for partnership at a large firm, a lawyer needs to have a stellar pedigree. Basic document review work is generally not considered to be professionally relevant skill-enhancing work for this professional track. Although Ginger was hoping to get back on track at a large firm as an associate, she could not land interviews or get any traction on her search. Recruiters told her she they would not be able to help her find any job prospects at any large firm because she had done document review for a year. It was 2010, and the economy was tanking, which made the search even more competitive. The only jobs she was able to interview for were more contract and document review jobs. Ginger was worried that she had ruined her prospects for an associate position.

Ginger went to a bar association conference to hear about other options in the law, and attended a panel discussion about in-house jobs for lawyers. One of the speakers was an in-house counsel who spoke about options for lawyers at her level of practice. After the panel discussion was over and the speakers were preparing to leave, Ginger approached the panelist.

At first he was very friendly and asked about her background. When he heard the law school she graduated from and the first firm where she had worked, he became very interested and conversational. She then gave him her résumé and he reviewed it. When he saw that she was currently doing document review contract work, his attitude abruptly shifted. He became negative and scolded her, saying, "No wonder you are having trouble finding good work. You should never have left your job for a contract position." After that sharp comment to her, he got very busy with his papers and essentially ended the conversation. Ginger was devastated, and after that, she shied away from networking until we met for counseling.

The panelist had appeared to be a possible wizard, but he turned out to be an ogre. Ginger felt at least temporarily defeated by his comments, and she let the incident interfere with her search efforts for a period of time.

It wouldn't be a heroic quest without a villain or two to deal with. In *Star Wars* Luke Skywalker had to deal with Darth Vader, but that did not stop him from his quest. Don't let the ogres of the world deter you from your mission. Unlike the prediction of the ogre she met, her job quest eventually led to a good position at a small firm where she was again on track for partnership.

A special problem can arise if you, yourself, are the ogre. If you devalue the efforts you are making and give yourself negative messages, you can put a stop to the effectiveness of your job quest. It takes energy and hope to conduct a job search. Negative messaging destroys energy and hope. If you are not engaged in an interpersonal, interactive search, then what is left? Sending more résumés to dragons at the drawbridge of the castle? Trying to create friendship without fully engaging with people in person? We already know that is not as effective.

Fortunately, knights and wizards are far more plentiful. Based on reports from my clients, I'd estimate that two-thirds of the people you will meet will be knights and wizards, and only one-third will be ogres, if that. In addition, knights and wizards are easy to spot using the Voice Test you will learn about later in this chapter. Your job is to find helpful people, because your search progresses as you go from one helpful person to another. That is how you get over the mountain, through the forest, and make it to the castles.

Who Are the Gatekeepers?

Every workplace has people who can help you get past the castle gates. They have the ability to get a job seeker recognized in the inner sanctum of the castle by the key keeper or other important castle staff. The gatekeepers sometimes do not realize that they have this power. They might just work in the castle or have a relationship with the castle's key keeper or someone else trusted by the key keeper, and because there is no official recognition of the role of gatekeeper, they may not think they have any power whatsoever. Sometimes a gatekeeper is a husband, wife, or other relative of someone inside the castle. Sometimes the gatekeeper works in a related castle or plays golf or is on a board with a key keeper. For that reason, if you ask that person to take your résumé to the person in charge of hiring, the response might be, "Sure, but I don't know if that will do any good."

It is important for you as a job seeker to recognize that, even if the gatekeeper is unsure of her clout, she might still be more of a trusted contact than she recognizes. So, ask the gatekeeper to introduce you to someone in the castle hierarchy if you know that the introduction will be positive. And coach the gatekeeper to help you by saying something good about you to those in the castle hierarchy if it is appropriate to do so. You are asking for an *endorsement*. But be careful to ask for that only if it is appropriate.

Endorsements can be strong or weak as we have learned, so it requires some assessment to determine if you want to ask for one from your contact.

A stronger endorsement has the following elements:

+ Your contact knows you, likes you, and knows your work (work product/work ethic).
+ Your contact knows someone in the castle hierarchy who is approachable and nice.
+ Your contact is willing to say something positive on your behalf to open up the opportunity for an in-person meeting.

If this gatekeeper you know asks, "Do you want me to say a good word about you when I talk with my friend (the key keeper)?" your answer is, "yes." Endorsements can be extremely powerful and helpful from people who are respected and trusted by those inside the castle. Endorsements help transfer the trust that the people in the workplace have in the contact person, to you.

Some people are well-versed in the ways of networking and need no coaching to volunteer positive comments about you. Other people are not as aware of the power of a few positive words to transfer trust. Endorsements are so important that it is better not to leave it to chance.

However, you never want to push anyone to give you an endorsement. Instead, say something that gives the gatekeeper the option to decline. For example, you might say, "I do not want you to feel pressured to do this, but if you are comfortable doing it, I would really appreciate it if you would say something positive to your friend X about my integrity, my work ethic, or anything else you have liked about my work you experienced when we served on that committee together."

In this way, you signal your gatekeeper that you would like support, but you also offer a gracious way to decline if it is too uncomfortable for your contact person to take that role. By modeling the comment you are looking for, you also help that person construct a productive endorsement that will open a door for you. Be certain to only ask contacts who know your work product to vouch for your work. Without that knowledge, they can only say you are likeable, which, although worthwhile, is a weaker testimonial.

Some people try to ask for an endorsement inappropriately from people who do not know them well or do not have a good sense of their work or work ethic or have not yet met them. LinkedIn is a resource to find connectivity into a market, but unless you meet someone in person and have a good experience in that meeting, an endorsement from a contact generated online will not usually be substantive. Asking someone to vouch for you or even introduce you before they have met you can be a serious mistake. The contact person might experience that request as an imposition. The introduction, if it is made at all, is likely to be unenthusiastic or doubtful. This is a situation where a job seeker has to use common sense and intuitive judgment. If you can find a way to do it, you want to meet in person, nurture a relationship, and have an informal interview that will help the listener understand why you would be good for the job.

Looking for Villagers behind the Castle

An example of finding gatekeepers to promote a job quest for a government position comes from a client who was a litigation associate at a large firm. He had graduated from a top-tier law school with excellent grades and had been an editor for his law school's law review. After graduation, he went to a large firm where he was assigned to the litigation group. He was expected to be an aggressive and confrontational lawyer, but he was more of a reasonable, thoughtful person by nature. Appellate work, with its emphasis on research, writing, and oral argument, was far more enjoyable for him.

In our work together, it became clear that a career move into a position with the federal government might be a good strategic and personal career decision for him. He looked at usajobs.gov, the website for federal employment, and learned of a number of job prospects that fit with his interests in appellate-based work. He prepared his applications.

He then launched a concurrent search for classmates who were working for the federal government in the Justice Department. One day while he was looking at one of the websites for one of the federal agencies he was interested in, he thought he saw in the background of one of the workplace photos the somewhat blurred image of a classmate from law school. He contacted his friend by e-mail and, sure enough, his friend was working at that agency. When he told this friend about his interest in a job at the same agency, his friend told him to shoot his résumé over and he would hand deliver it to the person in charge of hiring. He did that, and within about two weeks he was asked to come to Washington, DC, for an interview. He was hired by the agency a few weeks later and was very happy with that decision.

You could say it was lucky that he saw his friend in the photo, but it is more accurate to say that he had a hand in creating his good luck. He did that by actively hunting for people he knew in the village behind the castle and maximizing the chance when he did find someone he recognized. In addition, since he was also a bright, personable guy who had a good reputation in law school, he was able to get an endorsement from this friend who was connected to the keeper of the castle keys and also able to bypass the dragon.

Finding Gatekeepers in a New City

I had been working with an associate, Dorothy, who was an insurance defense litigator. She had been vacillating about whether to leave her law firm in the Midwest and move to Arizona. Her firm expected associates to work long hours and assigned a heavy volume of work but offered no real chance of eventual partnership. She was burned out doing insurance defense work and wanted to change practice areas. To make matters even more challenging, the recession was in full swing at the time she was trying to make this transition.

Dorothy went through the process of finding her career sweet spot. She identified commercial litigation as a practice area that she was excited about. She learned how to conduct a job quest, prepared a new résumé, and practiced her interview. But since she had no connections in Arizona, Dorothy continued to be indecisive about whether to leave her current job and risk a move without having a job in Arizona. One day, she came into my office and told me that she was sick and tired of being ambivalent. She had decided that she would quit her job and do what she had wanted to do for many years. She applied to take the Arizona bar exam, sold her condo, left her job, rented a van, and moved to Phoenix.

I did not hear from Dorothy for many months. When I finally did hear from her, I was delighted to learn that she had made a successful transition. She sent me this e-mail:

"I wanted to update you on my progress since moving to Phoenix at the end of February and thank you for your guidance in my job search! I will start work at P__ on Monday doing business/commercial litigation. I am thrilled about the job. . . . I employed your strategy for networking and getting interviews, and I think it was a great success, thank you! I had several connections here that I could exploit and, to your point, there were many people who were willing to meet in person and help out.

I got a lot of mileage out of a few meetings. It was easy to be positive about the search after having helpful people on board with my searching and making calls became easier over time. One place I interviewed laughed because I knew so many people around town (thanks to your method) and that I had people from all over advocating for me – even on the golf course!"

Learning how to connect with people who might be able to advance your search forms the basis for the productive search in which you employ rapid relationship and trust building. One of the best ways to do this is to have a lot of starter conversations that pave the way for you to advance your mission. Dorothy's success was based, in part, on her willingness to have many starter conversations after moving to Phoenix.

Where Will You Find Knights and Wizards?

The fastest way to find your knights and wizards is to join and participate in your professional community. Meet with people who live in the neighborhood you want to join. In the context of your job quest, think of the professional community or neighborhood that you are trying to connect with as the village behind the castle where tradesmen and

tradeswomen interact with each other and also know the people who live in the castle. You want to show up there and become known to them in a positive way. You also need to learn more about who lives in that neighborhood and what is happening there.

At times, you might feel as if you have become something of a groupie, learning who is a standout in your professional neighborhood and also trying to locate people who have recently joined it. You try to learn about who is contributing to the community even though you might currently be an outsider. You also want to learn about the hot topics for this realm.

How to Meet Knights and Wizards

One of my clients, a forty-year-old dissatisfied transactional real estate partner at a small firm, decided he wanted to make a fairly radical career shift into what was, at the time, the new field of information technology. He needed to learn the practice area in order to enhance his value to this new market. So he enrolled in an L.L.M. (Master of Laws) program in information technology. As part of his job search, we mapped out his strategy. One step was to get involved at the local bar association and very actively participate in the relatively new IT committee.

He got involved with that newly formed committee, helped set up committee programs and created relationships with the panelists as he put together those meetings. He also co-authored a cutting-edge paper in the field of IT law with one of his professors. In the process of getting involved in this newly forming professional community and creating a presence for himself, he was referred to potential clients, groups of young entrepreneurs with start-up companies who needed legal help but did not have a lot of money. The referrals came from his professor and from some of the more established lawyers he met who were involved in the bar committee. One of the entrepreneurial groups he counseled developed rapidly into a successful business and, following the career plan we had set up, he proposed himself as their in-house counsel. He prepared a business proposal and made a presentation to the company. When they accepted, he was thrilled. He had done what few lawyers are able to do late in a career, namely, transition laterally out of one practice area into a totally different area and land an in-house counsel position with an exciting new business in only about a year's time.

If you can find a way to interact with the community you want to join, you will enhance your luck, especially if you create a positive buzz about yourself in that neighborhood.

What are people in this industry talking about? You can gain a lot of this information by reading local business magazines and trade publications, participating in professional association committees, and checking bulletins for events scheduled by professional associations.

You can also talk with professionals who live in the village or who are traveling through the forest. As you find your way through the woods, advancing from trusted contact to trusted contact, you will meet new knights and wizards through the knights and wizards you already know. You can find many more people to connect with by having a series of starter conversations.

What Is a Starter Conversation?

With *starter conversations,* you reach out to your close contacts first and then to people your contacts suggest – knights and wizards – to find out if they will be helpful to you. It is important for the success of your search that you have a great many starter conversations. In healthy economic times, my clients usually need to have about 20 to 40 good starter conversations and in-person meetings to learn about job prospects or potential opportunities in the industry or market they want to pursue. This number varies and depends on the field, the job seeker's level of expertise, how robust the workflow is in the target market, and how the job seeker presents himself, messages, and advocates as he encounters people in the industry.

One of the best ways to begin this process is by connecting first with your closest friends, relatives, teachers, and others who are in your circle of professional and personal contacts and try to find anyone, even someone who is tangentially connected to the target market or industry. If there is someone you already know who is in any way connected to the castle or the village behind the castle, send him an e-mail or make a phone call to start the process. The person you contact may be married to someone whose cousin works in the castle. The person you contact may be retired and no longer live in the village behind the castle, but only a few years ago had many contacts in that village and still has some good information about who is important there and which workplaces are good for you.

If you start with an e-mail, try to set up a phone call so you can hear the person's voice. This is important because of the voice test that we will talk about in a minute.

Call the contact and engage him or her.

First, introduce yourself and give your connection to the person you are calling. The connection needs to be either a person in common or an experience you share. You never want to make a cold call.

If the connection is a person in common, the introduction can sound like this:

> "Hi, my name is Travis, and I am a friend of Brad Davis. Brad suggested that I call you and said you'd be a really helpful person to ask for advice and information. I hope I am not calling you at a bad time, but if I am please let me know. I would be happy to set up another time to talk with you if that is possible."

If you have an experience in common, the introduction might sound like this:

> "Hi, my name is Dan, and I don't know if you remember me, but we were on the same fundraising committee" (went to the same professional school or same undergraduate school, have kids in an activity together, belong to the same club, etc.).

The rule of thumb is that if you had some sort of friendship or working relationship in the past that satisfied the threshold level of friendship, it is usually fine to assume those people will remember you in a positive way, especially if you remember them in a positive way as well.

Second, tell the person why you are calling (your dilemma/problem).

> "I am at a crossroads in my career."

> "I am trying to figure out some things having to do with my career."

> "I am trying to learn about what is going on in my professional market."

Some additional helpful information includes:

> "I am looking for advice, information, market knowledge, market intelligence, and/or insights."

> "I am hoping you will brainstorm with me."

You can add:

> "And, by the way, I am not calling to ask you for a job."

Third, give the person a glowing synopsis of your background. This is your résumé. Say good things about yourself. Be succinct. Do not use jargon. Even your best friends do not really know what you do, so you have to give each contact a snapshot of your skill set and experience. Talk as if you are communicating with a smart ten year old. You can say, "I hope you don't mind if I tell you a little bit about myself so you are in a better position to advise me."

Fourth, describe what you are looking for (your castles). This is where you put your workplace prototypes to use. The prototypes or ads are your description of the types of workplaces that you have determined would be a good fit for you given your skills and the market need.

> "I am looking for small cutting edge companies where I can develop software."

> "I am looking for small, respected litigation boutiques."

> "I am looking for non-profits where I can use my skills in development."

Then always add:

> "I am interested in places that are busy, active, growing, and have a good reputation, meaning that people like working there."

In other words, you are trying to find the castles for which you have written a prototype, and you are asking your contact to help you to identify the places that fit the description you give your contacts.

Fifth, ask people to turn on their mental computers. If you have more than one type of workplace that would be good for your skill set and career goals, then walk your contact through the description of each one. Do this methodically, one by one. You never know who your contact person knows, so do not presume to know that the person can only connect you with one type of village or castle.

Even if the information you are seeking could be obtained via Google or some other resource on the Internet, do not rely solely on the information you gain there. These interactions lay the groundwork for relationships that are crucial for your networking success and for success in marketing in the future. As people assist you, you create and deepen *friendship and trust* relationships.

At this juncture, you are hoping that the contact person will identify places that fit the description or multiple descriptions of the workplace(s) you are looking for. If you have done your homework, you may have heard of these places already. If so, see what more you can learn that will advance your search. Your conversation may go something like this:

> "Can you think of places that fit the descriptions I just gave you?"

> "Have you thought about Sprout Social? How about Uber? Or I think I heard that Google is going to be opening up a branch in the city."

> "Yes, I read about that company in Crain's. Do you know any of the people over there? Do you know someone nice over there who might be willing to talk with me about the firm and what they do? If you are comfortable doing it, I would really appreciate it if you sent the person you know an e-mail to explain who I am and that I would be contacting him to get advice and information so I don't end up in the spam filter."

Sixth, try to meet in person. At some point in the process of having this conversation, you should try to change the meeting from telephone to in-person. It may be best to do that fairly early in the conversation. The time to transition to an in-person meeting is when you realize you have found a knight or wizard, which you can tell from the **voice test**. We will cover the voice test the next section. If the voice test tells you the person you are speaking with is a natural counselor, then you want to try to meet in person.

Here is a good transition line to encourage an in-person meeting: "I don't know if you have the time to meet with me in person, but the information you are giving me is so useful, so helpful. I wonder if I could buy you a cup of coffee (or meet for breakfast/ lunch/dinner or in your office) so we could keep talking. Would you be willing to do that?"

The person will either say yes or no. If it's no, you can continue to talk over the phone. If the person says yes, you have just landed an informal meeting. This is not a formal interview, of course, but an in-person meeting may open the door to a more formal vetting process that can lead to a job at this workplace or another one. For that reason, it is important to think of every meeting as an interview. Each meeting is a chance to make your case and advocate for yourself, as well as learn more about the marketplace for your industry and on-the-ground information that can help you become the insider. The person who is willing to meet with you in person is usually a natural counselor, a knight or wizard, a helpful person. How can you figure out if the person on the phone is a natural counselor? The answer is the voice test.

What Is the Voice Test?

You can usually identify a knight or wizard by his voice in the first few minutes of your starter conversation. A knight's or a wizard's voice goes up in pitch. An ogre's voice goes down. This is the *voice test*.

When you talk with a person who engages with you, you can hear it in her voice. When a person engages with you, she starts to think along with you. She might say, "Oh, you should talk with my friend, Nick," or "I know just the person you need to meet!" You can hear that engagement in the pitch and tone of the voice as well as the content. By contrast, the affect of the ogre is flat and low. "Well, I really don't know who you should talk to. I just don't think I can help you. I just don't know of any jobs." Think of Ben Stein's voice or Eeyore from *Winnie the Pooh*. You can tell the level of engagement from the conversation's content as well.

Because the sound of a person's voice is so important when trying to figure out who the helpful people are, e-mails are not as effective for locating knights and wizards. You cannot hear the affect, pitch, or engagement in the contact's voice in an e-mail exchange. E-mail can, therefore, be misleading or simply opaque when it comes to finding natural counselors.

What Should You Do Once You Have Found a Knight or Wizard?

In-person meetings with the knights and wizards of the world are very important for a successful job quest. To illustrate this point, let's use a 10-point scale, where 10 is the highest:

- It is a 10 to meet in person with the natural counselors of the world, the knights and wizards. Even if they are simply in the same neighborhood you are trying to become a part of, they might know a lot and can also spread the word about you and help you to become part of the neighborhood buzz.

- It is a 5 to talk with someone over the phone without any further contact.
- It is a 3 to communicate only by e-mail.
- It is a 1 to send something by snail mail if you could be meeting in person.

Why is meeting in person so important? It increases the level of engagement and interaction that is crucial for a productive networking search. The in-person meeting is your chance to really talk with someone who is in the village or connected with the castle. You can hear more of the gossip and rumors. The person cares about you more once you meet face-to-face. You can create greater trust. You can take advantage of the communication conveyed by body language and voice.

Remember, the in-person meeting is actually an interview. The person who meets with you will, hopefully, go back into the work world neighborhood and talk about you behind your back, which is just what you want her to do. To find a job through the grapevine, you want to become part of the grapevine and the buzz that goes on in the work world all the time.

I have a friend who worked for IBM and was engaged in product development with Japanese companies that IBM might want to partner with to produce new products. Even though Japan is a long way away, he was often in Japan or flying to or from Japan when he worked for this company. One day I asked him why he had to travel to Japan so frequently. Why not use videoconferencing to connect with his potential clients there? He replied, "There is no substitute for shaking someone's hand and looking him in the eye to create trust."

This is true for your job search, as well. You are also in sales while you are networking to find a job. You are promoting yourself as a valuable asset. Just as a sales professional needs to show up in person to create trust, in a productive networking search, you are creating trust relationships that can help to open doors for you in a number of venues. You are also creating trust relationships with many people in the village who then assist you in finding your way to the castles you have described to them. More magic happens in person. People are memorable, paper is not. By doing your quest in person as much as possible, you are creating and enhancing your luck and good fortune.

Assemble Your Virtual Round Table

Part of creating your own good luck is creating a team of people who are advising, supporting, strategizing with, and counseling you. Think of them as the board of directors for your search effort, or the knights who join your virtual round table. If you can find people who will be on your team and are willing to be sources of information and support for you, it can advance your search efforts.

Who do you want on your team? It depends on what you are trying to accomplish in your search and where you are in the arc of your career. If you are a new graduate, you want to enlist your professors, past bosses, partners, or others who have been impressed with your work during your summer jobs, internships, or externships. If you are further along in your career, you should be able to enlist your current bosses, coworkers, past bosses, people you have served with on committees and others who see you in a positive light.

You will also find new knights and wizards for your virtual round table as you create new trust relationships. You want to include people who are connected to your targeted neighborhood, the village where you want to find work, and the castles you are trying to connect with. Career counselors and career services professionals might be good people to add to your team as well. The team you put together will never sit down as a group, of course; they are simply members of a virtual round table that help you to have a successful quest.

Your Laptop and Cell Phone Are Your Travelling Research Buddies

Even though your computer can be tempting as the primary way to find postings and create relationships, we know that in-person meetings and on-the-ground information are crucial for rapid relationship and trust building. This does not mean that your computer or your cell phone should be put in a closet to gather dust. They are wonderful, amazing tools for information and research. They should be your close companions on your quest. Do you want to know if jobs are plentiful in your target market? Do you want to learn more about hot topics in the field you are trying to join? Your computer can tell you that. Do you want to learn more about someone your co-worker mentioned who moved to a new job in a comparable company? Are you looking for a friend of a friend who is doing the job you wish you were doing? LinkedIn, Google, Facebook, blogs, websites, and apps can all help you to navigate your journey by providing valuable information and insights about your target market and the people who are in the realm. There is even a new app for professional interaction and networking called Bond (getbond.co) that helps professionals get together and meet up, as well as learn tactics and skills for relationship building.

Chapter Seven: How to Get Knights and Wizards to Meet with You

You have begun your adventure. You have entered the forest with an idea of the places you want to explore and the people you want to meet to find your way to the castles.

- *You prepared well.*
- *You are contacting possible knights and wizards by phone and e-mail.*
- *You are having a lot of starter conversations.*
- *You are using the voice test to find the natural counselors.*
- *You are always approaching a contact through another trusted contact.*

You understand how important it is to meet in person with knights and wizards. But how do you get a busy knight or wizard to meet with you in person?

What Do You Say?

THE STARTER CONVERSATION reveals the natural counselors of the world who will engage with you, the knights and the wizards. It also reveals the people who will not engage with you, the ogres. The

90

voice test is the key to that quick determination. Once you make that determination and you find a knight or a wizard, you know you want to try to meet in person if possible. The more direct and honest you can be the better, while also being mindful of the contact person's busy schedule.

Here are some examples of how to start:

"I am learning so much from you. I have no idea if you would be willing to meet with me in person, but it would be great if we could do that and keep talking. If you are too busy to do that, I understand, but if you could find the time, I'd really appreciate it."

"The information you are giving me is so helpful and so useful. Could we get together in person? I'd be happy to meet for breakfast, lunch, dinner, or coffee, or meet at your office. Whatever works for you."

When Do You Say It?

Within the first few minutes of your starter conversation, you will usually know if the person you are speaking with is engaged with you. If she has joined with you to brainstorm, to address your dilemma, to offer suggestions of places and people, now is a good time to try to convert the telephone conversation into an in-person meeting, if possible. You'll need to rely on your intuitive judgment and common sense to determine the optimal timing. You should be able to figure out if this person is being helpful or not. Trust your response based on the way that person is interacting with you. The voice test is the single best simple litmus test of another person's connection to your cause. So listen for the voice that goes up in pitch and the affect in the voice before you suggest an in-person meeting.

Why Does This Work?

There are three main reasons why the knights and wizards of the world will agree to meet with you in person.

First, you have been referred by a **trusted contact** of theirs. The positive connection that the contact has with that trusted person transfers to you and paves the way for your connection. When you are referred by a friend or business acquaintance of theirs, the contact person wants to stay on good terms with that business acquaintance. In part, the contact person might meet with you as a favor to his friend. The underlying reason matters less than the fact that you have gained access to a knight or wizard. After that, it's up to you to make a good impression and learn about what you need to know.

Second, you have used the **voice test** to find someone who likes advising and counseling others and who gets pleasure and enjoyment out of that. The natural counselors of the world are personally enriched by helping others. The process of assisting another person feels good and brings satisfaction to them. If you are someone who likes helping others, you already know this basic truth. If you are not that kind of person, maybe it's time to re-invent yourself.

Third, the knights and wizards of the world have figured out that helping others is a way of life that is important for career success and for success in life. By helping you out, they are helping themselves out as well. Helping others is ultimately a somewhat selfish thing to do because it engenders a willingness and motivation for you to repay the favor someday. Maybe you will provide an important business contact. Maybe you will help her find a job. If someone has helped you out when you needed that assistance, you will want to give back. What goes around comes around. Organizational psychologist Adam Grant of the Wharton School writes about the value of **generosity** and helping others. It is good for the giver as well as the person receiving the assistance. The givers of the world are over-represented among the most highly successful people on the planet. This is true as long as the person can also establish appropriate limits. The article "The Saintly Way to Succeed" by Susan Dominus in the *New York Times Sunday Magazine* addresses this concept quite nicely.

Super Wizards

There are some people who are so well-connected and so central to the professional realm where you are trying to find work that they can help your job search be even more productive and rapid. They can do this because they know more people and understand the industry well. These people are super wizards. They are usually easy to spot because they are very active and engaged in the realm. They usually have a lot of contacts because they are friendly and collegial. Why would a busy super wizard spend time advising you? Just as with any wizard, the reasons have self-serving as well as altruistic aspects: perhaps his friend asked for that meeting, or the super wizard really enjoys advising the next generation, or she knows that what goes around comes around. Someday you might provide guidance for her son or daughter or even for herself once you are established in your career or your new job.

Never feel as though your time with a super wizard is an imposition. Super wizards are able to stand up for themselves and tell people when they are too busy to meet. They will let you know their time limitations. In addition, there are gifts you can give a super wizard who spends time helping you. These gifts cost you nothing other than some time and a little energy. One of my clients, a new graduate from Notre Dame, was hoping to land a job at a prestigious law firm in Chicago. He had coffee with a partner from that firm and then he mentioned that as part of an alumni event he was going to a football game with a high profile, in-house counsel from a certain company who was also an alumni of the school. The partner got excited about this and said he had been trying to get a meeting with this in-house counsel for a long time. He asked my client if he would be willing to connect them up. My client did that for the partner and the partner was very grateful. A few months later my client landed the job as an associate at that firm. The partner confirmed that he was happy to promote my client because he believed he could be a valuable asset to the firm. "It's rare to see a student who is this comfortable with networking," he told my client. Gifts of information, support, connection, promotion, and help are valuable gifts that we will learn more about in Chapter Nine: Friendship Lite.

What if They Won't Meet with You?

Sometimes people are just too busy to meet in person. If the contact person is not a close friend or a friend of your close friend, he may be less interested in meeting with you in person. If the contact person is an ogre, you will not meet with him face-to-face. Sometimes, despite your best assurances that you are not going to try to push your new contact to give you a job, he is wary and may think that you do, indeed, have that unstated agenda.

If the contact person is not interested in meeting with you face-to-face, or is not able to do so, you can still learn valuable information over the telephone. If you engage that person's help over the phone and then give her something to show you are grateful and thank her verbally, you might convince her that you are someone who can be trusted and that you are worth helping. The gifts you can give do not need to cost you anything other than time. Even if you are unable to give your contact person a gift, thanking her verbally for help may be sufficient. People who are willing to help others are rewarded and gratified when they are asked to take the role of mentor, as long as the person looking for assistance does so in a thoughtful way. You always want to be mindful of your contact's time constraints and express your gratefulness for any assistance.

What to Avoid Saying and Doing

Once you have found a knight or wizard using the voice test, you know you have found a contact person who enjoys engaging with and helping others. You never want to take advantage of someone who is willing to do that. One way you might create a problem for yourself is by becoming a pest. If you call back repeatedly to ask for advice and information, or if you e-mail constantly for feedback and guidance, you run the risk of losing the contact person's support.

You want to elicit the contact person's advice and learn what that person has to offer you, including the names of additional contact people. You want to thank him and give him a simple gift of information, promotion, connection, or other support and move along on your quest. Every time you interact with a contact person, try to make the interaction beneficial for your contact. Always think about what you could do to make that person's life better in return. You can occasionally circle back with additional questions if they arise and you really need to reconnect, but be careful not to wear out your welcome. If this wizard is willing to join your virtual round table, you can ask for more advice from time to time, but always be careful not to overdo it.

When you engage another person to ask for assistance, it can be a mistake to use a pretense or a bogus reason to set up a meeting. Say, for example, you learn that the person you want to meet with is deeply involved in a nonprofit organization that has a mission of helping inner city kids learn how to play squash. You do not know the first thing about squash, but you pretend that you are interested in the sport and engineer a "chance" meeting at an exhibition squash match. This falls into the category of pretense, and if your lack of knowledge or interest becomes obvious, it could be embarrassing and possibly damage your quest.

However, there can be occasions for creative networking if there is an authentic shared interest. Say, for example, you have done triathlons and plan to do more of them, and you learn that the wizard you are hoping to connect with does them too. If you learn that he is going to be helping to organize and run a triathlon for a favorite non-profit, it is good creative networking to volunteer with the event and through that link find an opportunity to meet up with that wizard and deepen a connection. One word of caution, though: it has to be authentic.

Pretense or dishonesty in your early interactions with contact people can affect the level of trust you gain or lose. Ultimately, the quest is about creating trust relationships and gaining a positive reputation in the community in which you want to live for the rest of your career. This is not about gaming the system. The last thing you want to do is create a negative buzz in this neighborhood you want to join. People are smart. Wizards and knights did not get to be wizards and knights without having good instincts and emotional intelligence.

The Confidentiality Issue

If you are conducting a networking search, you might be justifiably concerned that the buzz you create in your professional neighborhood could get back to your current employer. The way to minimize this potential problem is to tell everyone you talk with that you really need to keep this conversation confidential. Say it four times. First, say it at the beginning of your conversation to set up your meeting. Second, say it in the beginning of your conversation in person. Third, say it at the end of your in-person conversation. Fourth, say it in your thank-you e-mail.

What do you say? "I just want you to know that it really could be a problem if my current workplace/boss hears about my search. I really hope you can be extremely careful to maintain confidentiality."

In my practice, clients who have inoculated their networking conversations in this way have not reported a breach of confidentiality. The downside of this approach is that there may be a less expansive buzz created in your professional neighborhood. If the person you are entrusting with your search secret is a known gossip, then avoid him if confidentiality is your highest priority.

On occasion, when a job seeker has voluntarily told his or her employer about doing a job search, the surprising result was that the employer offered a more attractive deal to get the job seeker to stay. This is a situation that requires reliance on your intuitive judgment, including the leverage you have at the workplace and the way coworkers have been treated previously when they conducted job searches at this workplace.

Can You Make Your Meeting Happen Using LinkedIn or Facebook?

Online sources of connectivity can be very helpful. If you can start a conversation online and develop a relationship there, by all means you should do that. However, if you think that the person you have met online really knows you, likes you, and knows your work only by interacting with you online, that is probably an overestimation of your connection. The most effective way to turn an online friend into an endorser is to meet in person if possible. The reason has to do with the way people communicate. Since much of what we convey and how we feel close and connected to other people occurs through body language, including voice inflection, tone of voice, the way you look and move, as well as eye contact, it can be a problem to rely solely on social media for relationship building. Using Skype to create a closer relationship is better than social media alone, but you still have a personal disconnect. You interface with a camera, not with a flesh and blood person in the same room. You can see someone's reaction but it is not as interactive as when you are in the same room together. You may develop a relationship via Skype, but you do not maximize the potential for a deeper connection. Certainly, there are times when you cannot meet in person. In that case, Skype or social media could be your best option. But if you can find a way to meet in person, you have a greater opportunity to maximize the magic that turns into job search luck.

Chapter Eight: What Happens in Meetings with Knights and Wizards

You are on your job quest to find your way to castles your research indicates could be good matches for you. You are calling your closest knight and wizard friends, and through them you learn about other knights and wizards who will guide you through the forest. You e-mail them or call them and have starter conversations. Some of the people you talk to have agreed to meet with you in person. You want those meetings to go well. These contact people have the potential to:

- *Guide you through the forest*
- *Help you locate other castles and other helpful people to talk to*
- *Tell you where the workflow is stronger*
- *Help you fulfill your dream and solve your dilemma*
- *Help you to meet the castle gatekeepers and key keepers*
- *Join your round table as a coach and advisor*

You need to know what to say, what to ask for, and how to help your contacts to help you.

Create a Comfort Zone

You are about to meet in person with a knight or a wizard. You have already had a brief conversation by phone or have interacted by

98

e-mail or on LinkedIn. You have told this person that you are at a crossroads in your career and looking for guidance and information. This person has already started to help you in that brief interaction or conversation. You realized that she was a wizard, so you converted the conversation to an in-person meeting and now you are going to have that meeting. How do you start?

Start by creating a **zone of comfort.** Start small and look for commonalities. It is usually easiest to talk about neutral subjects like weather or if the person has ever been to this restaurant before or a mutual friend or a mutual experience or an interesting piece of jewelry that the person is wearing or some other innocuous topic of conversation. You want your contact to feel comfortable talking with you. If you have researched these possible commonalities before you meet using LinkedIn, Google, and other resources, you can guide the conversation to something you already know you have in common.

Even though you are talking with this person in a business context, it is fine to talk about lightly personal things, like family or shared interests, such as golf or other sports, art, the theatre, fashion, comedy clubs, dogs and other pets, or some other pursuit. Additionally, you may enjoy some small talk about a charity or not-for-profit, hiking, vacations, or holiday plans. You could also have common interests in professional organizations or activities. None of these topics is overly personal or highly charged. They serve to create a comfort zone for everyone and form the underpinnings of a casual business friendship.

Once you have created that comfort zone, though, you want to move on to some important topics that will help you with your quest.

Move into Biography

Once you have created a comfort zone, you can move into a conversation that includes your contact's background. You can ask how your contact got where he is today and learn about his career choices. Most people like to talk about themselves. If you ask for your contact's story, he will be happy to talk about the evolution of his career and you can learn a lot from that history. You can learn a lot about what works and does not work in the context of a career in the same industry or field you want to pursue. When you learn someone's **biography**, you also hear about this person's way of thinking and his choices and why he did what he did. All of this is valuable information. In addition, you can ask questions and get clarifications, which is not possible if you read a book or an article about an industry.

Ask open-ended questions. For example:

"How did you get into this field?"

"What do you like/dislike about it?"

"If you had your career to do over again would you still choose this career path? Why or why not?"

"Who seems to do well in this field? Why do you think that is?"

"Who seems to get ahead at this particular company or firm? Why is that?"

"What do you wish you had known before you started this career?"

"What are five things about this career/job that surprised you?"

Biography can teach you a lot, but if you are conducting a job quest and not just informational interviewing, you cannot limit the conversation to biography. Informational interviewing is done to learn more about an industry to see if you are interested. That is crucial to identify the right career direction. But once you are on your job quest, do not get stuck in biography. There is a great deal of ground you want to cover in a short period of time, so it is important to move on from this topic.

When do you move the conversation to the subject of your job quest?

This is another moment when you rely on your intuitive judgment and some magic words.

Talk about Your Dream and Dilemma

It can be challenging to try to move the conversation from small talk and biography to the topic of on-the-ground advice and information about the market and workflow that you really need to gain. One of the best ways to transition to that phase of the conversation is to say something that turns the conversation to your problem and the reason why you are meeting with this person:

> "It sounds like you have been able to create a terrific career for yourself in this field. I am hoping to be able to do something similar. I have a dream, you could say, and a dilemma (or a goal and a problem). One of the reasons I wanted to meet with you is to tell you my goal and to get your advice about how you would accomplish this goal if you were me, given what you know about the field."

Since you are meeting with someone who is a natural counselor, asking for advice engages your wizard in a topic that is bound to be interesting to her.

Be an Investigative Reporter

The best way to conceptualize your role in the in-person meeting at this juncture is to think of yourself as an investigative reporter. Your job is to find out what is going on in the forest and in the castles. You need to find other people to talk with. Investigative reporters are not shy about asking questions that will give them accurate and up-to-the-minute information. They need to get the story, just as you need to. They need to create relationships to get to the next source of information, just as you need to. Here are some questions you might ask:

> "Here is my résumé. Where do you think a person with my skill set might be valuable in the current market in this industry?"
>
> "Do you know of workplaces that are busy and growing?

"Why do you think they are busy?"

"How do they look for people to hire at the workplaces we are talking about?"

"Do you know who is in charge of hiring at the places we are talking about?"

"In this field right now where do you see the greatest activity?"

"Given my goal and problem, do you have other ideas or advice for me?"

"Do you know of affinity groups or professional groups I should join or blogs or other publications I should read?"

"I have a list of people I would really like to learn about or meet if I could. Here is that list. Do you happen to know any of these people? If you do, do you think any of them would be nice enough to be willing to talk with me and provide advice and information as you are doing?"

"If you do know of more people who are doing the work I would like to be doing, how would you recommend that I contact them to learn more? Just to be clear, I would not be asking them to find me a job."

"Would you be willing to send an introductory e-mail to connect me with your friend so I don't end up in the spam filter?"

"I have a list of places that I would really like to learn more about. Here is the list. Do you know what's going on at any of these workplaces in terms of how busy they are?"

"Can you think of anyone else I could talk with to get advice and information about people and workplaces in this industry where there is some indication that the places are busy and growing?"

As you ask these questions, the answers you get from the contact person will lead to more questions you will want to ask to open up productive areas of inquiry for your search. Be sure to add your own questions to this list of questions.

Know How to Turn the Meeting into a Job Opportunity

There are some important ways that your mission is different from that of an investigative reporter. Unlike a reporter, the story you are investigating is about you, namely, "How does a person with my skill set and background fit into the current market?" This story has deeply personal relevance for you.

In addition, the person you are interviewing may possibly be vetting you at the same time. The person you are talking with is learning about you and your aspirations and seeing your résumé and advising you. Your contact is learning about what you are looking for and trying to brainstorm with you to figure out where you could find opportunities. Together, you are on a mission to help you find the right career direction and/or busy workplace that might yield an opportunity.

Your contact knows that your goal is to find job opportunities. So, without ever mentioning *jobs*, this contact person will be considering whether you would be a good fit for her workplace. For this reason, if you do have an interest in the contact's workplace, you should speak up and say so. If you do not say anything, the contact person might conclude that you are interested in other workplaces but not hers. You need to quickly assess whether the contact's workplace sounds interesting to you and whether you truly fit the criteria for landing a job there.

To do that, apply the **Formula for Getting Hired:**
1. You have a **skill set match**.
2. The workplace has good **workflow**.
3. There is likely to be a **culture fit** based on what you have learned.
4. You can come to the attention of the workplace through a **trusted contact**.

If you are interested in the workplace and you do fit the criteria, then speak up. Here is what you can say:

> "I have no idea if your workplace has a need for someone with my background, but as you were talking about where you work it seemed like it might be a pretty good fit.

I wonder if it would make sense to talk to whoever is in charge of hiring. Who is that?"

If you find out this information, you have discovered the key keeper. Ask your contact, "What do you think about meeting with the person in charge of hiring for this kind of position. Does that sound like a good idea to you? Could that be arranged?" If the workplace is relatively small to mid-sized, this may be the way they find their new hires. If you can meet the key keeper even before the workplace has a need to hire or has posted a notice online for someone with your background and you stay in touch with people at that workplace, your chances to land the next job for someone with your background will be far better. Even if you have to apply through normal channels and face the dragon at the front gate, you may have created a relationship that will help you move past the dragon. Who knows, you might even have successfully recruited yourself to your future workplace.

Help Your Contact Person Help You

As we already know, many job seekers conduct their networking searches by asking everyone they can think of if they have heard of any jobs. A more effective way is asking for advice and information, trying to meet targeted people in the right neighborhood, sharing your dream and dilemma, learning where the workflow is stronger, building relationships and giving back. You want to go to the meeting with the agenda of learning. Because so many people network by asking for jobs, many contact people you encounter will assume that you are only interested in information about current job openings and whether their workplace would want to hire you immediately. As we have learned, that leads to a response that is too brief and not helpful enough for your purposes. For that reason, if your contact person says something like," I don't know of any jobs. If I hear of something I will send you an e-mail or call you," be sure to gently redirect him to answer the questions you are asking. Try saying something like this:

> "You know, what I am most interested in learning is any on-the-ground information, including speculation and rumors about what is going on in this industry and this group of firms and companies that are experiencing

growth. I do not know enough about the market yet. I need to learn more. I hope I am not imposing on you too much by asking you so many questions."

It is your job to keep your contact person on course, providing you with the information you really need. Help your contact person help you. Guide him back to your questions, and do not let him end the conversation without learning more of the information you need to have to enhance your luck.

Always try to find more wizards and knights, because you never know where the opportunity could come from. As you venture further away from your close connections, you have more chances to hear information that goes beyond the "low hanging fruit" your close connections have already told you about.

Give Back and Be Generous

Since the information you seek takes time and effort on the part of your contact person, you want to be mindful of that and thank your contact for helping you. Arguably the single most important aspect of your networking search goes beyond landing your job. The most important aspect of your effort to find work is that you create trusted contacts in the neighborhood you want to belong to for the rest of your career. You are creating new friends. These relationships can open doors for future business and future jobs. None of the time and effort you put into this process of relationship building is wasted time. Some of the people you meet will be on your virtual team, supporting you and helping you find opportunities. Many will become closer friends over time. You owe it to your contacts to assist them, too. You want to return the favor if you are able to do so.

How can you do that? Business friendships are not necessarily close, personal friendships, but they do need to be authentic. Status may be an issue. For example, the senior people who counsel and guide you – the wizards – may not be your peers. How do you help them out, especially if you are just beginning your career? You may not think that you are in a position to give them important information or advice in return but that is not true. That brings us to the concept of *friendship lite*, which we will explore in the next chapter.

Chapter Nine: Friendship Lite

You are meeting with knights and wizards and telling these natural counselors your dream and dilemma, providing a clear picture of what you are seeking, asking for guidance, learning on-the-ground gossip and rumors about the workflow and places that are busy, active, and growing, and you are showing people your master list of people and places and finding more knights and wizards. These people have taken time out of their busy lives to counsel you. What can you do to thank them for their help? That is what "friendship lite" is about.

What Is Friendship Lite?

THE WIZARD OR KNIGHT you meet with is a person you have asked for guidance in a business context. This contact may be a teacher; a current or past boss; a coworker; a person who attended your professional school or your undergraduate school; a friend of your father, mother, or other family member; or a manager who has seen you at work. By using a starter conversation and the voice test, you have uncovered the natural counselors. When you engage the help of a natural counselor, you are creating a relationship. The relationship may or may not evolve into a full-fledged social friendship in which you get together after work, go to social events together, share personal information, or meet extended family and friends. What you often begin with is a business friendship.

A business friendship should be a two-way street. You get, and you also give. It may not be purely a one-for-one give-and-take in which you closely tally the score, but you do want to give back if you have gotten a benefit. This is part of friendship lite.

One of the surprises of friendship lite is how easy it can be to create this kind of relationship. It is not a deep or intense relationship. It is based on a comfortable interaction in which you help the other person feel good about interacting with you. Friendship lite is a brief, positive interaction that has the potential for long-term growth.

The degree of continued social connection can also be affected by the status of the person you are interacting with. If you are just starting your career and you are connecting with a person who is older and more established, such as a boss or a professor, you may be less likely to develop a social friendship out of the networking meeting. The more senior people in a realm are usually the wizards. They have often taken the opportunity to develop deep connections in the community you are trying to join. You do want to try to meet with as many wizards as possible, because they are usually very knowledgeable about the market, the workplaces, the workflow, and more. They may be friends of the gatekeepers and key keepers who are also from the same age group, having worked their way up in the ranks in their field. But the relationship will be affected by a person's status. If your boss or your professor is significantly older, that generational difference might affect the degree of social interaction that evolves from your networking meeting. These and other social factors might influence the degree of social connection stemming from your networking.

However, when it comes to having a business friendship, age does not need to be a barrier. If you can help someone older than you or younger than you be successful in a business context, you want to try to do that.

Why Friendship Lite Is Not an Imposition

The minute you pick up a phone to call a knight or wizard or send an e-mail, you are starting a new relationship.

If you are concerned about bothering the person you are about to contact, or you think that what you are doing is an imposition, you will probably never even make the connection or call. It is true that you are asking a stranger to give you time and advice. And if a total stranger called you and asked you to move furniture or paint a fence with him, you would probably not want to do that. But your request for advice and information is different.

First, you have vetted people to find the natural counselors. These are people who like to counsel and advise others. What you are asking these people to do is something they enjoy. It is not as if you are asking a total stranger to move furniture with you or paint your fence. Your request is like asking a book lover to go to a book fair or a football fan to go to a game with you. The person enjoys the activity you are inviting him to do.

In addition, you have been introduced by a trusted contact. You are not a total stranger making a cold call. A mutual friend is the go-between. Because of that connection, you benefit from the extension of good will from one friend to another. *Trust transfers.* We will discuss this concept more in Chapter Twelve: Four Overarching Concepts. You are getting the reflected positive feeling from that friendship. This is generally true even if your relationship with the trusted contact is only a limited level of interaction that could be thought of as "friendship lite."

Meeting with you will take time. Knights and wizards are very busy people. In the context of the quest, these professionals are usually racing around on their chargers, dashing through the forest on their way to business meetings, social events, and professional lunches. If a knight or wizard spends time with you, you want to be sure she does not regret it.

How can you repay a knight or a wizard?

How to Give Back

Good Deeds

You can give simple gifts to people who are good enough to spend time with you and help you. These gifts do not have to cost a lot. Some of them will only cost you some time and a little effort.

There are gifts of **information, promotion, connection, attention, volunteer help**, as well as **inexpensive tangible gifts.**

A Gift of Information

Providing another person information can be a wonderful way to give back. The information a contact person needs could be work-related or more personal in nature. For example, perhaps your contact just lost a nanny and you know of a good nanny service; that could be valuable information for your contact person. You could send an e-mail after your meeting to provide your contact with the website or phone number of the nanny agency you used to find a wonderful caretaker. Additionally, if you can think of a good book, website, or blog to help your contact person get needed information, you can provide that by e-mail.

Books can be good gifts. They convey information and are also tangible gifts. Write your thank-you note in the flyleaf.

One of my Chicago clients, a trial lawyer, was trying to network his way to a job in New York so that he could move there to be with his fiancée. Brad knew a very well-connected super wizard who was high up in government in New Jersey and they had a conversation over the phone. In that conversation, they talked about their love of dogs. Both of them loved schnauzers and they had a terrific time talking about why their dogs were so special. Brad then sent this wizard a coffee table book about schnauzers and wrote a note in the flyleaf thanking him for taking the time to talk with him. The wizard e-mailed him a thank you and included three contacts in New York. My client then contacted these people and set up a trip to meet with all three of them. The meetings went very well, and as he was boarding the plane back to Chicago, one of the people he had met with called to offer him a job with their boutique litigation firm. Brad moved to New York and has been very happy with the choice he made.

Other clients have provided their wizards with varied, yet useful, information: a good restaurant in Mexico City, a good book or movie, the best hybrid car to buy, the best ride share service to use.

Providing useful personal and professional information is a gift.

A Gift of Promotion

Most professionals need to develop and maintain a positive image in their professional communities. Writing and speaking are two good ways to develop and maintain a presence. If you are in a position to help your contact person develop and maintain a professional presence, that is also a gift.

If you co-chair a professional association committee, for example, and you are able to offer your contact person the opportunity to speak on a panel or at a lunch meeting, contribute to a webinar, contribute an article to a journal, or write a piece for your blog, that will help your contact person's professional career.

Giving your contact the opportunity for professional recognition is a gift.

A Gift of Connection

Professional careers thrive on meeting new people. If you know someone who would benefit from meeting this new contact person, help both people by connecting them with each other. You can simply send an e-mail introduction to each person giving the background of each to the other and why you think they ought to meet each other. You might connect two people by having them both join you to do something together, like go to a sports event, go to the taping of a show you found out you all like, or go to a professional meeting together.

Here are two separate examples of introduction e-mails:

"It was wonderful to spend time talking with you about restaurants that might be interested in the wine I import. I learned so much. After our meeting, I thought of a good person for you to meet. He is also developing a new restaurant and is facing some of the same challenges you mentioned when we met. I am sending him an e-mail to introduce you. I hope the two of you get together. I am certain you will enjoy meeting each other."

"I would like to introduce you to someone who could help you connect with that company you would like to work with. The two of you should meet. The three of us could go out for drinks after work. I'll set it up if you like."

Connecting people who could benefit from knowing each other is a valuable gift.

A Gift of Attention

Listening – truly listening – to someone is a gift. These days, it is rare for a person to have uninterrupted time to talk, to express a concern, or to tell a story and have another person's undivided attention. It is rare for a person to get the opportunity to talk without having the other person preach, dictate, or prescribe action. Having "air time" to convey thoughts and ideas, to speak openly and honestly, is rapidly becoming a casualty of modern day life for many people. We may be more plugged in to electronic devices, such as cell phones and computers, but often that communication is more of a sound bite, a rapid exchange of information, a "tweet," not a leisurely conversation. Face-to-face interpersonal interaction is not as prevalent in general. Who is really listening to anyone else these days? A simple willingness to listen and affirm another person is a gift.

Give your contact person the gift of being heard and supported.

Attentive listening means asking a question and letting the other person answer without interruption and then asking follow-up questions to encourage more talking. It also means being supportive, empathic, affirming, and nonjudgmental. You want to have good eye contact and turn off your cell phone or other devices.

Ask open-ended questions to be supportive:

"How long has this been going on?"

"What have you done so far to try to help?"

"What resources have you looked into?"

"Have you thought of using a support group?"

Be empathic:

"That must be hard for you to deal with."

"I'm sorry your dad has developed this problem."

Be nonjudgmental:

"How did your son get involved in this kind of problem?"

"How is this affecting you?"

It may be that the person you are talking with does not want to engage in this kind of conversation. That's fine. Never push it. But if your contact wants to discuss a problem at work or even a problem with a family member, such as a daughter who has just had a DUI or a problem finding a nursing home for her mother, you should encourage the discussion. The person may need the "air time."

Paying attention is a gift these days.

Volunteered Help

If your wizard is involved in a cause, such as a political party or a not-for-profit and if you genuinely share that interest, volunteering to help that cause can be a great way to interact more with this person. One of my clients, a trial lawyer trying to develop business at a large law firm, had a somewhat tangential connection with a very well-known wizard who was playing a central role in the election efforts of Barack Obama in 2007. By volunteering to help this person raise money for Obama's campaign, he was able to create a lot of good will with this very central person. Although that did not directly result in business right away, it did result in connections that created business and eventually resulted in a new job through another very central wizard in the not-for-profit world that he met through this volunteer work.

A More Tangible Gift

Sometimes it makes sense to spend a few dollars to send a meaningful tangible gift to a contact person who has spent time with you and helped you. It could be a card with a handwritten note or something more.

One of my clients, a new graduate, had a very helpful networking lunch meeting with a woman who was in the same industry. In the course of their conversation, they talked about recent vacations they had enjoyed. The wizard had just returned from a trip to New Orleans where she had discovered she liked jazz music. They connected around this topic. The new graduate had been a fan of jazz for many years. To thank her contact for spending time talking with her, she downloaded music of her favorite jazz artists onto a disc and sent it to her wizard with a note thanking her for her time.

> "Thank you for spending time with me. I learned so much
> from you. When I heard you say that you had discovered

jazz on your trip to New Orleans, I put together a CD you might like with some wonderful jazz artists who are my favorites. Hope you enjoy it!"

Tangible gifts should be small and based on a person's interests that you learn in your face-to-face meeting. Books are great gifts. If you learn that your contact enjoys mountain climbing, skiing, salsa dancing, travel, or is raising a child or training a dog or engaged in some other activity, buy a book or send an article or a link to a site that reflects that interest. Thank you notes that are handwritten are small gifts, too, especially if you go to the trouble of buying the card from an art shop or art museum.

When to Thank Your Knights and Wizards More Formally

When you network for information and advice and develop lite friendships that have the potential to be more substantial friendships, there can be times when the lines of formality and informality blur. For example, you meet a knight or wizard to discuss what it is like to work at a smaller company. In the process of that meeting, you learn that the workplace is in need of a person with your background, so you ask to be considered by the company. That information changes the way you interact with the knight or wizard going forward. The relationship should become more formal. In this case, you would not send a handwritten note and small gift, because that would take on the appearance of impropriety. It might look as if you are trying to influence the person you have met to hire you by sending a present to him or her. If you are being considered for a job, every interaction should be formal and documented. Communications should be in writing. Gifts are not appropriate when you are being formally considered for a position.

Chapter Ten: Interviews

As you have been building relationships and working your quest on your way to job opportunities, you have already been engaging in interviews. In your encounters with knights and wizards, they have asked why you are leaving your current job, what you are looking for, and what you are trying to accomplish with your career. Each time a contact person asks you these questions, you have the opportunity to advocate for yourself and use the opportunity to learn more about what is happening in your target market and at the specific workplace where your contact person works. These meetings are mini-interviews that can open doors for you. They are discussions that could lead to your new job.

THERE ARE THREE MAIN TYPES of interviews that occur in a job quest:
+ Informational
+ Informal
+ Formal

Be prepared to advocate for yourself in an effective way in each of these settings. Prepare for the meeting not only by knowing your own background well, but by having an overarching story that helps people you talk with understand what you bring to the table and how your whole work history has led up to the reason you want this particular career/job. Know the traits most employers look for and be ready to talk about how you have those traits. Prepare anecdotal evidence or stories from your past that support the general statements you will make about yourself. Use the comments of others who liked your work to bolster your assertions that you make about yourself. Understand how to create good "music" in your interview. And if you anticipate tough questions, think through how you will deal with them and help the potential employer to be reassured that you can do the job that needs to be done.

The Informational Interview

As you work your way through the woods and encounter knights, wizards, and the occasional ogre, you are trying to meet with wizards and knights in person. The conversations you have with these contact people are often called "informational." You are learning. You are interacting with these people to gain important information for your search. You need to hear about the lay of the land, and you also need to create relationships. Where is the work? Who are the key players in the realm? Which castles might have an interest in you, given your background and your skill set? Who is the keeper of the castle keys?

As you gather this information, you are creating new friendships, deepening existing friendships, and creating trust relationships. You are also actively engaged in helping the knights and wizards you meet by providing them with gifts of information, promotion, connection, attention, and volunteer help, as well as inexpensive tangible gifts. By the time you have met with or at least talked with 20–40 of these contact people, you could probably write an article on this topic: where are there good opportunities for work for a person with your background and skills in this particular professional community? You are learning about the castles you think match up with your skill set and learning about the identity of the key keeper as well as hearing the gossip about these workplaces.

The informational interview can rapidly turn into an informal interview and, on occasion, can shift to a formal interview as well. This can happen if the knight or wizard meeting with you realizes that you could be an addition to his workplace. This can happen most readily if the wizard or knight you are meeting with is a gatekeeper or the keeper of the castle keys.

It can also happen if you realize you are a good match for this castle, and you suggest that you could be useful by saying the key words that shift the meeting from informational to informal interview:

"I have no idea if your workplace would have an interest
in someone with my background but would it make sense
to start a conversation with whoever is in charge of hiring?
By the way, who is that person?"

The Informal Interview

An informal interview is a meeting in which you are being vetted for a job but the setting is more casual, and the agenda may be lunch or a meeting in someone's office and a seemingly casual conversation. Sometimes, that lunch turns out to be an initial interview and the beginning of a vetting process for a job. The informal interview can happen during a job quest when the person meeting with you in an informal setting has an interest in vetting you for a possible job but does not tell you that up front. There can be many reasons for what might seem to be a lack of candor. The person meeting with you may not have the authority to hire, but has the power to suggest candidates. The person meeting with you may not be sure you will turn out to be a good prospect and needs to meet with you first to make that threshold determination. There may not be well-defined job prospects at his workplace. There may be no posting on the website or anywhere else. Until the vetting person meets you, there is no way to know if you are going to be the right person to bring on board. As a result, sometimes there is a little dance that people do around the interview. It is termed an informal meeting or just lunch, when it can be more than that.

Another possibility is that the person meeting with you might initially believe she is just helping to inform you about the market, but by the time you are done with lunch, if you are impressive enough, she may be trying to figure out a way to bring you on board because you are just too outstanding to pass up.

From the job seeker's perspective, it doesn't matter whether the meeting with the contact person is billed as an informational or informal interview. The way to approach such a meeting is *as if* it is an interview. You want to be prepared to advocate for yourself and present strong answers to questions you are likely to be asked at any stage of the networking process.

Sometimes, a job will be created for a person who networks effectively into the hidden job market, makes a good impression, and has the right core competencies for a workplace that is busy and growing. This is true especially when he is ready to advocate for himself in an informational or informal meeting.

Sometimes there is no job at the time of the meeting but soon after a need does arise, and the job seeker is on the radar because he had that informal lunch that made him known to the castle.

The Formal Interview

The formal interview is the interview that people tend to think of as the "real" interview. This is supposed to be the one that counts, and for some castles, that may be the case. If you apply for a position using more formal channels, as you usually need to do with a large firm or company or the government, you might land a formal interview. However, as we already know, if you use the Internet to approach most workplaces, you have to get past the dragon at the drawbridge to get to a formal interview. Depending on the workplace, an informational or informal interview that brings you to the attention of those in charge of hiring might be every bit as important as the formal interview, because these are the vetting exercises that get you to the next level of scrutiny.

At times, in fact, the formal interview may be pro forma. This can happen when you make it through the informal meetings where the tough questions are asked and answered well. By the time you reach the formal interview stage the only real question left might be whether you fit into the workplace culture and how much you will cost the workplace if you are hired. You have already been vetted by key people for your skill set and passed that test.

In short, it is important to be prepared for a good interview as soon as you set foot outside the cottage and begin your quest.

Be Ready for the Interview from the Start of Your Quest

The difference in the preparation for informational, informal, and formal interviews is simple: there is none. Once the rest of the equation is met – the work is there, your skills match or are close enough, and you have a trusted contact or credible endorsements – it usually comes down to good energy or interactions that are comfortable and how much you will cost if you are hired.

Because the casual meeting can shift to a probe of your skill set, background, and professional knowledge, whether you indicate your job interest or not, you need to be ready for your interview as soon as you start your quest, before you meet your first knight or wizard.

Your Overarching Story

Why do you want a career in this industry? Why do you want a job with this company? What can you say about your past work that helps the potential employer understand why you are choosing to go in this career direction or search for this kind of job? Your overarching story needs to help the people you meet with to understand what you are looking for and why you are seeking it.

Recently I worked with an attorney who wanted to move from the law into higher education administration. He had been working in the field of law for ten years. He had recently been working at a firm where he did mostly document review and appeals, which was not interesting or challenging for him, and he had no desire to continue in the practice of law. After conducting an assessment using AIMS and AILS, and the Essential Elements exercises in this book, it was clear that he was excited about working in a more interactive work setting, putting together events that people enjoyed going to and where he might someday help to shape policy. Mark was a graduate of a large Midwestern university, and his experience at that school was one of the highlights of his life. Because of his love of the school, he had volunteered to be the local alumni relations club coordinator in the Chicago area and had been thoroughly enjoying that work for a number of years. Because he liked the work so much, he was a standout in that volunteer job. The volunteer position allowed him to do many activities he did not have the opportunity to do as a lawyer, which included motivating, training, and collaborating with volunteers as well as conducting marketing campaigns. He developed positive relationships with people in the university alumni office, and they could see that he was doing a good job at developing alumni connections in the Chicago area. Because of his connections with the alumni office, he heard about a job at the school. They needed a Manager of Regional Relations for the Alumni Association Office. He would need to be willing to move, but he was able and willing to do that.

What followed was a campaign to be hired that we worked on together and that included how to message effectively to tell his story to the hiring team. He also needed to change his résumé to translate his skills so that the employer would understand how he could be an asset to the Alumni Association, despite having been a lawyer for many years. He was able to make his case by pointing to his ability to communicate well, supervise and train people, and work with clients in a service industry. The overarching story was very important. He also talked about how he had a long-standing passion for the school and that had been the motivation for his involvement with the alumni club and his avid support and engagement with alumni relations activities. This messaging was carried through his cover letter, his résumé, and his communications with his wizards who stepped up and vouched for him. He carried that messaging through in his interview. Mark landed the job and could not have been more thrilled.

It is not easy to move from one field to a totally new field without re-credentialing. His success was built on his volunteer activities and his passion for that work, but the overarching story mattered as well.

The Importance of Anecdotal Evidence to Persuade

The interview is your opportunity to advocate for yourself. Just as the relationship building phase is about friendship, the interview phase is about advocacy. It is an opportunity to help the potential employer understand how you could be a valuable addition to the castle and to help the potential employer feel reassured that you are a good choice for the job. To prepare for an interview, think about the potential employer's needs. Ask yourself what you would want to see in a candidate's skill set and background if you were the employer. If you can figure out the employer's needs, you can prepare for your interview more effectively. Check the company or firm website. Try to read articles about this workplace. See if you can find people to talk with who once worked there, especially if they worked there recently. You can sometimes find these people using LinkedIn or a directory of professionals in your industry in the city where this company is located. You can also talk with people who work at comparable places where the skill set is likely to be similar.

Just as you may be nervous about landing a job with this employer, potential employers are also nervous. Unless they have worked with you before, they have to develop some degree of confidence that you will be the right person for the job. What if you do not turn out to be the kind of wonderful employee you say you are? Anticipating the concerns of potential employers is important. They need to be reassured that you will be a good hire.

You accomplish this by producing solid evidence that supports general statements you want to make about yourself. When it comes to the interview, your evidence is anecdotal.

When I ask clients, "Why would you be a good hire for this position?" a typical answer usually sounds something like this: "I am a hard worker, and I always give every job I do 110 percent," "I am bright and capable and intelligent," or "I am very responsible."

These answers are conclusions. They are general statements. But they are not yet good advocacy. Conclusions are unconvincing. Why should the listener believe what you said? How does he know what you say is true? What is the evidence?" If you can only come up with conclusions, you will not have a convincing case.

The way you marshal your evidence for the interview is in the form of anecdotal material. If you hear yourself saying something that is a conclusive statement, such as "I am a hard worker," then you need to force yourself to supplement your answer with supportive anecdotal documentation, such as the following.

> "I have a long history of being a hard worker. When I wrote for the *Michigan Law Review*, I not only edited

my own pieces, but I routinely stayed until 2:00 a.m. the night before submission to the printer to review all of the articles for typos or errors. I am still the same today. Just last week we had an emergency motion, and I was the one who stayed overnight to be sure everything was done perfectly before we filed the next day. I don't mind doing that. I truly love doing this kind of work, and it's important to me that the work is done at the highest level."

"I am a good account manager. I say that because I work really hard, and I have a good ability to understand and work with clients of all kinds. For example, when our company had a very difficult client to work with, my boss asked me to assist him working with this client. I got along well with the client even though he can be very demanding. The account has grown 30% over the last two years, since I started managing it. The client always asks for me to be the one working on his account."

Remember that the anecdotal material must be honest. There is no exaggeration allowed. If you have done a good job in the past, there should be no need to pretend to be anything more than you are. In fact, you want to assert the truth about your level of performance and skills, because if you land the job, you will be expected to perform at that level. If you disappoint your employer, that could mean poor reviews and even eventual job loss.

Bring in the Comments of Others about You

In the interview you can talk about what other people have said about you. If your boss or a client has said great things about you, you can and should quote or paraphrase what they said. It sounds less self-congratulatory to have a third-party comment about you than for you to praise yourself. It is more credible to the listener to hear: "After we finished the trial, the client wrote a letter to my partner saying he had never seen a more dedicated, bright associate and asked to have me included on the trial team in any future matters."

Know the Traits Employers Want

What other anecdotal information should you prepare for your interview? As you think about what a potential employer would want from a person doing the job you are hoping to do, identify the key elements you would look for from that worker. Here is a partial list of typical traits and skills that employers like to know you possess:

1. Loyalty
2. Energy
3. Perseverance
4. Attention to detail
5. Honesty and truthfulness
6. Ethical standards
7. Ability to research, write, and understand industry concepts
8. Street smarts
9. People skills
10. Ability to work on a team
11. Ability to follow directions
12. Willingness to put in long hours when that is needed
13. Likeability
14. Real enjoyment of the work
15. Good judgment

For every one of these traits, you should prepare short stories from your past that illustrate that you possess these traits.

One great way to find out the list of traits that an employer would like you to have is by having an informational interview with someone in a comparable job. By doing that, you will find out what the person believes one needs to be successful in a position that is similar. Take notes. Then prepare your list of traits to prove up using your background as evidence.

Another way to discover this list of sought-after traits and skills is to find a posting or ad for a comparable job and see what the job requirements are, write out the list, and identify the evidence that you can point to in your experience for each trait or skill. It is good to quantify results that you have gotten. Include numbers and the size of the project. For example, if your agency has received 30% of their revenues from your efforts as a project coordinator, be sure to say that.

Just keep in mind that ads and website postings will not mention the personal, intangible characteristics that may be important factors for landing the job: factors such as an ability to get along with other people on the team, maintain a good disposition, or work well with a micromanaging boss. Yet, they may be the most important traits for landing the job.

You can address these unstated material requirements by anticipating that your personal qualities matter to the interviewer. You can give examples and illustrations of how you work well on a team, maintain a good attitude under pressure, or work well with difficult and demanding bosses by using anecdotal material that establishes those points in your interview.

How do you know if the workplace is interested in certain personal qualities, and how do you know which ones matter? If you have networked your way to the key keeper, you have already been hearing about the workplace. You have heard about people in the hierarchy and the culture of the workplace, the gossip about the workplace, and the good and bad news about some of the people who work there. Networking is the best way to learn about these intangibles that can be extremely helpful to you when you prepare your case to be hired.

Be Ready to Advocate for Yourself

In a typical interview, you will be asked questions that you will need to answer, but you also have a core agenda that you want to advance. While you are answering questions, you are also trying to work in your key points.

Your core agenda in the interview is to answer the question, "Why should we hire you over the competition?" If you can answer that question by identifying the reasons you will be a great choice for this job, you have the basis for the advocacy argument that you need to make in your interview. Write out the answer before you go to any interview or before you call the gatekeeper or the knight who could help you get a formal interview with the key keeper.

It is not always possible to get your entire advocacy message out in response to one question, but you want to be determined to get it all out there at some point before you shake hands and say goodbye. Keep your key points in mind. As you make your points in the interview, you can check them off your mental list of things to be sure to say. Of course, you want to repeat them succinctly in your thank-you letter.

Be the Expert about Your Own Background

It is a given that you should be knowledgeable about your own background and skills. In addition to the dates and chronology of your work history, you also need to be able to speak comfortably about every matter, deal, and project you allude to in your résumé. You need to be ready to answer the question: "What was the most difficult situation you have dealt with? What did you do about it? What happened when you did that? What did you learn from that?" Be sure you identify what you did and what your role was. It can be tempting to say "we" did this or "we" did that, but the listener then cannot tell specifically what your role was. You want to be clear and specific. "We worked as a team of four on this project, and what I did was put together all of the displays for our company, organize the timing of the events, and prepare the brochures that every participant received." That will help the listener understand your involvement and contribution.

Know Your Value in the Marketplace

Once you have convinced the key keeper that your skills are right and that you will fit in, the issue of compensation has to be addressed. You have to know your value in the marketplace and your value to this castle specifically.

Learning compensation levels is easier if the workplace is one that is well-known to recruiters or is a governmental entity. A boutique or smaller workplace will not be as likely to have published pay scales. The way to find out what other professionals make at these workplaces is to conduct a few informational phone calls or e-mails to ask friends or people you locate through LinkedIn at comparable firms or organizations what the acceptable pay range might be. Never ask what your friend actually makes.

The compensation dance can be tricky. If you are asked what you want to make early in the vetting process and you answer but your expectations are too high compared to others with comparable skills or too high compared to what the workplace is ready to pay, then you can be summarily removed from the interview process and lose your chance to advocate for yourself. If you happen to come in too low, you might be considered a less stellar candidate, or you might be hired as a bargain but feel cheated and disappointed when you learn what you make compared to others in similar jobs at the same or similar workplaces.

The discussion of compensation is best when you know the employer really wants to hire you. You can tip the balance in your favor through creating good rapport with the interviewers. It can take some time to do that, which means that you try to develop that good relationship throughout the interview process and delay the discussion of compensation until rapport is built. One way to postpone an early discussion about compensation is to say, "I care a great deal about the work I will be doing and the people I will be working with. If we agree that I am right for the job, then I am absolutely certain that we will come to a meeting of the minds about the level of compensation. But there are some things I would like to discuss first before we get to that question."

What could make this topic trickier are economic concerns, which should be factored into your assessment about when to talk about compensation. If you play hardball in a recession, you might lose out to another candidate. Is this job one that is important to you as a stepping stone to the right field or to add needed skills? Then you might want to take it, even if the pay is not what you want it to be. To maximize your chance to obtain the highest possible level of compensation, try to build a rapport with the interviewer and delay the compensation dance. When you attempt to postpone this discussion, watch the interviewer's reaction. If you sense that you are disappointing the interviewer, and if you are concerned that you will be throwing away a job you really want or need, try a different tactic. Say, "I would be interested to know more about how this company handles compensation, and I would like to learn whatever the current compensation level is for people with my skills and background. What would that range be?" Be open to the needs of the workplace, but also know your personal limitations and your bottom-line salary requirements. Assess your career goals to see if it could be worth it to take a job with the potential to give you other benefits, even if the pay is not what you hoped for.

There are also situations that require you to identify your compensation level early in the process. For example, if you are working with a recruiter, it will waste everyone's time if you are not able to identify your salary range. Give the range you want but add that what matters most is the job and people you will be working with. Salary requirements do not need to be a deal breaker if the job is right in other ways.

If you answer an ad and it requires that you state your salary requirements, you may have to do so to get to the next level of scrutiny. This is another reason why online ads have limitations for job seekers. It is almost impossible to respond with full or nuanced answers, unless you can communicate behind the scenes to someone who is advocating for you inside the workplace.

Understand How to Create Good Music in the Interview

The question of whether you will fit into the culture of the workplace is the "music" between you and the castle staff that is vetting you for a job. This is not just the schools you attended, but how comfortable it is to talk with you. Do you have shared interests with the interviewer or with potential coworkers? Are you pleasant to have around even if you don't have much in common with others? Decisions can come down to personalities clicking, and it is something that you do not have much control over. It is generally not even directly mentioned in the interview. No one is going to say something awkward like: "Will we enjoy working with you? Are you someone who will work well with our team?" However, you can be certain that is what your interviewers are wondering when they conduct the interview. Typically, a key keeper and others involved in the interview process assess that fit factor by seeing how you act in the interview.

If you get terribly nervous in an interview, you might say something that is disarmingly honest, such as, "You know I really am excited about this job, and I feel pretty nervous right now about this interview because

I would really like to work here." That might help the interviewer to feel good about you even if you seem uptight.

Sometimes it helps to imagine that the interview is taking place in your home and you are the one welcoming the interviewer into the place where you live. Pretend you are having a party and the interviewer is your guest. You want the interviewer to feel welcome. Instead of thinking about how nervous you feel in your interview, this device might help you adopt a frame of mind in which you are helping yourself and the interviewer feel more at ease.

Making a good connection in the interview is one of the single most important intangible aspects of your quest. That is one reason why it is usually a good idea to include interesting hobbies and community activities on your résumé. Sometimes a shared hobby is the key to having a lot of fun in your interview and helps you land the job you have worked so hard to find.

Manage Tough Questions

When you are on a job quest, you meet many new people, and they may ask why you are searching for a job. If you have been fired, that might be a question you would prefer not to answer for fear of embarrassment. Most professionals are high performing type-A people, who have had many successes in life and will have many more in the future. Being let go may be the first disappointing event of your career. It is normal to be worried about talking with people who will ask why you are leaving your job. Should you tell the truth and say, "I was fired," or should you try to pretend it did not happen? Some professionals who have been fired are so unnerved by the experience that they avoid interacting in person on their job searches to circumvent uncomfortable questions that could lead to an admission about being let go. When faced with a direct question about outplacement, some people lie about it and say they were not fired.

This is not the best approach. Castle staff, gatekeepers, and key keepers at the castle where you are interviewing might have back-channel conversations with villagers, castle staff, gatekeepers, and key keepers in other castles in which they could learn the truth about your situation. If that happens, your candidacy is more likely to be in jeopardy than if you had told the truth from the beginning. If you have been fired or outplaced, you have to be ready to handle questions about that, because the uncomfortable questions are going to come up eventually, not just from friends, family, and others who are trying to help you, but also from gatekeepers, knights, wizards, and the key keeper when you meet for an interview. You must prepare for that and any other dreaded questions. You want to have a consistent statement so you are not tripped up by back-channel conversations about your reasons for looking for a new job.

It is usually best to address the issue realistically and without pretense. Deal with uncomfortable questions by planning what you will say and practice with friends and family. If you have been let go, your attitude about that event is probably the most important part of your answer. If you convey confidence that you will find another good opportunity, that you have learned from this experience, and that you see this out-placement or termination as a positive career move that could result in something better, that positive attitude will have a good effect on the interviewer. You want to be careful not to say really negative things about a former boss or workplace. You never know who knows who. The person you are saying bad things about might be closely connected with the interviewer. Tread carefully.

In a recession, there is no reason to define an outplacement as a personal failure. Many companies and firms experience a significant reduction in the amount of work they have to do when the economy is not growing. Decisions about which staff to let go will often be dictated by a perceived overabundance of people at a certain level or a need for a group to cut back generally because there is a lack of work in that particular area. Decisions to fire workers during difficult economic times are often made with great reluctance since the company has invested time, money, and effort recruiting and training these workers. Your company's lack of work was not the result of your job performance. In a robust economy, the same people would not have been let go. There is no reason to feel ashamed.

Simply explain that you are one of many people leaving the company or firm as part of an economic shift that many firms and companies have experienced.

"I'm one of ten associates and partners who has been let go by the firm. Our firm has been deeply affected by the current economy. The firm had to downsize."

Then reassure the potential employer by urging him to talk with wizards who endorse you at the workplace you are leaving.

"This is an economic outplacement. I was assured of that by the manager I work with most closely. I want you to call him so that you can hear about the excellent work I did."

Some of my clients are surprised to discover that when they talk honestly about being let go with people who can advance their job quests, they receive great support and warmth. When job seekers can admit that they were fired or outplaced, they're likely to receive greater encouragement and assistance from the people they encounter. Some people are genuinely surprised by the degree of empathy and engagement they experience when they confide in total strangers as they network for new opportunities.

Stay on the Radar but Don't Be a Pest

Once you have found a prospective castle or cottage, try to stay in touch with someone inside. You can connect with your contact person, who may be a wizard, a knight, a gatekeeper for the castle, castle staff, or the key keeper. You can stay in touch with your contact person by e-mail and express your continued interest. Have coffee with your contact every so often if that is comfortable. Be generous when you can be. Connect people with each other. And use your intuitive judgment about the extent of your gifts of connection, promotion, listening, helping, and providing information. The idea is to stay on the radar screen as a person who is likeable and has a skill set that is valuable to the castle so that if and when they develop a need, they are thinking about you to fill that need.

Throughout the interview process, remain vigilant. If you do not know much about a given castle because you have not done much research on it, you may be concerned that it is not what you are looking for. Keep in mind that if it is the wrong workplace, you should be able to figure this out by checking information you learn about this workplace against your Essential Elements. By using your template to measure the workplace for your personal needs, you are vetting the castle for your unique requirements. Even if you have questions about the workplace or are not sure the workplace needs help yet, go through with the interview, because it could turn out that you are at the right place at the right time. Or the right place and right time could turn out to be a week or a month away. You are improving your luck.

Chapter Eleven: The Tipping Point and the Campaign Phase

There comes a time when you have enough information to know that there are a number of workplaces that might be job prospects for you. This is the tipping point.

How Do You Know When You Have Reached the Tipping Point?

You HAVE REACHED the tipping point when the elements of the Formula for Getting Hired are met: 1) there is a skill set match, 2) the workplace has good workflow, 3) there is likely to be a culture fit based on what you have learned, 4) you can come to the attention of the workplace through a trusted contact, ideally with an endorsement.

Once you have these elements, you are on a campaign to be hired. Even if you only have the first three out of the four elements, you could be ready to start a campaign to be hired. The tipping point occurs when you are ready to target particular workplaces you have learned about as prospects. It is important to identify this shift in your thinking, because if you are not certain about the way you view the workplace, you might end up inadvertently giving a key contact person the impression that you are not interested in that contact person's workplace. This is comparable to the difference in the way you would talk to someone about dating or talk to someone about marriage. If you are still in a dating mode, you will be more likely to want to find out about other people to meet. If you want to get married, you better not talk about other potential partners, because that conveys the wrong message.

You may have identified one castle or you may know of a number of castles where you are ready to meet the keeper of the keys. The tipping point occurs somewhat unpredictably as you conduct your quest. You might discover early that a particular place would work well for you, but there may be a dozen more castles that will emerge as you keep building relationships. What that means is that you still need to keep up the quest. When you do find a castle you like, start your campaign for that workplace and continue your quest with others that you are still unsure about. Use your Essential Elements template to be sure the workplace matches your needs.

Why You Can and Should Use the "J" Word Once You Reach the Campaign Phase

When you reach the tipping point, you can use the "J" word. You can talk about your interest in a job at a particular castle and be direct about it with the knights and wizards, villagers and gatekeepers you encounter on your quest because you know where you want to land; you know you fit the profile of the kind of person the workplace likes to hire, there is workflow, and you want to come to the attention of the castle staff through a trusted contact if you can find a way to do it. Using LinkedIn and other online resources can help you locate people connected with the castle that you can try to meet with. If you are likeable and have the right skill set, you might earn the endorsement of the knight or wizard who is connected to the target workplace.

The Endorsement and Why It Is Important

The campaign phase of your job quest is a concerted effort on your part to dig deep and find people who can connect you with the gatekeepers and the key keeper to try to meet with them. You want to come to the attention of the workplace through trusted contacts, people who have credibility with the workplace you are excited about. This takes effort. You also want to make a concerted effort to elicit and gain valid *endorsements* from your supporters.

We know what makes a good endorsement.

1. This person knows you, likes you, and knows your work and work ethic.
2. This person knows someone in the castle or a gatekeeper for that castle.
3. This person is willing to vouch for you to someone in the hierarchy of the castle who has or may have influence.

Sometimes people who could really assist your campaign to be hired do not realize how important endorsements are to your success. These people might not think to ask you whether you would like them to vouch for you to the castle staff or the key keeper. If that is the case, do not be shy about asking for their help and explaining what you hope they will do to assist you. Ask for an endorsement when appropriate.

Try to choose the right people to endorse you. There may be people who will agree to help you, but you might not benefit very much from their assistance. Choose people to do this important job for you based on their relationship to the workplace you are trying to connect with but also based on how positive and articulate they will be about you to the castle staff. Try to land endorsements from people who have good relationships with the key keeper and gatekeeper. Remember the qualities of a strong endorsement. A person who does not know you very well will not be able to give the most accurate picture of you to the key keeper or gatekeeper. Be careful not to ask a person who does not know your work for a recommendation that would include material knowledge about your work ethic or work product. Choose your endorsers carefully.

For example, if you ask a friend of a friend to say something good about you but that person has never met you in person, you cannot expect to receive a credible endorsement. The cure for this attenuated relationship might be to meet in person over lunch or coffee and give the individual a chance to interact with you. That informal interview might convince her to introduce you to the key keeper and be more enthusiastic. The in-person meeting that functions as a mini-interview can help the endorser feel more certain that you are worth endorsing.

The level of trust you enjoy from an endorsement can be an extension of positive feeling from the endorsing person based on membership in an affinity group. For example, if you are a University of Wisconsin graduate and you find a supportive manager at your company who is also a University of Wisconsin graduate, who likes you and is willing to vouch for you and help you to meet some of his classmates, goodwill from your contact can transfer to you. You are a member of a trusted group. The same is true for other people with connectors into the workplace, such as professors who liked the research work you did for them, the judge you clerked for, the lawyer who ran the legal clinic at your school, or the head of the community service fundraiser you worked on.

If you have done good work in your student and professional lives, there are people who have been impressed. Now is the time to ask them to rally to your support. It is as if you are running for office and you ask your supporters to give you a hand if they are comfortable doing that. You are asking your supporters to vouch for you to their extended groups of friends and colleagues. Of course it helps if the person is in the same industry in which you are trying to find work.

Social networks such as LinkedIn can be helpful. However, as we have learned, you cannot rely solely on an Internet friendship to elicit endorsements, because the level of trust is so attenuated and impersonal. People who can strongly endorse you have interacted with you in person, seen your demeanor, observed you under pressure, watched you solve problems and make judgment calls, and they have liked what they have seen. Whether it was the recreational hockey team or a volunteer project or a committee or your college classroom, if you made a good impression, it counts.

Ideally, when endorsers talk about you, you want them to speak from their "real time" experience with you. If you do not have that level of relationship, you should try to create some measure of trust by meeting in person for breakfast, lunch, dinner, coffee, or in someone's office, to help this person get to know you. That connection is the equivalent of a strong informal interview, which can create support for your bid in your job campaign. That good impression includes giving back to your knight or wizard.

Can You Start at the Tipping Point without Conducting a Quest?

If you are working with recruiters who find opportunities for you, you will jump over the quest phase and go immediately into the campaign phase. If you have sent a résumé in response to an ad and the dragon passes it along to the key keeper, you will go right into the campaign phase. Some people even begin their quests with enough knowledge to jump to the tipping point. They can bypass much of the quest. They might know this information because they have already been living in the neighborhood or they once were or are now part of the village surrounding the castle. It can also happen through the assistance of a powerful and friendly wizard who is willing to share her network with you.

Another way to jump to the campaign part of the quest is via a website posting. If you believe that your skill set matches or surpasses that of comparable candidates or people already working at targeted castles, you can try accessing the websites of firms and companies that your preliminary research indicates would be good matches for you. See if they are posting new jobs that require your skill set or skills that are reasonably close to yours. Some workplaces will talk with you strictly on the strength of a website submission if you are a great match for the skills they need.

As we already know, it can be very helpful to have people in the castle who have met you and like you and who readily endorse you. That means that even if you approach a workplace via the website posting, some effort to build trust relationships in the realm can turn out to be helpful to your candidacy. Many of my clients who conduct job quests and have built rapid relationships are excited to discover that one of the interviewers at the workplace is someone he or she already met and had coffee with on their quest. They might attribute it to luck, but really, it is engineered luck. Being known to the person on the hiring team can be very valuable.

Although it might seem logical that over-qualification – having more experience than requested or more variety of experience than requested in the ad – ought to be favorable for your candidacy, in fact the opposite may be true. The concern might be that you will need more money or that you will not fit in well in the work group. When assessing your match for the workplace needs based on the website posting, be aware that more may not be better when it comes to years worked or experience gained. Nonetheless, if your background is close, you should apply and make your case in the interview.

What Do You Miss Out on If You Skip the Job Quest?

Developing Relationships with Knights and Wizards

When you jump immediately to the campaign phase, you miss out on all the knights and wizards you could have met on the road, with whom you would have created trust relationships and friendships that could lead to a stronger network for your future and marketing potential for a long-lasting career in your field. For anyone who needs to develop relationships for business, the job quest approach is a wonderful way to launch your future network for business development, future job search, and professional development.

Learning Inside Information about the Market and Workplaces

If you go directly to the key keeper, you will have an interview, and in that interview the key keeper and others, such as recruiters, will portray the workplace in a positive light. "Everyone is happy here. We all love it here." That information might not be accurate.

By conducting your own quest, you will learn more inside information. The keeper of the keys might, for example, be a micromanager or a screamer, but she will not warn you about that and neither will a recruiter.

For example, the company may be seeking a new hire because the boss overseeing the group has rage attacks and regularly demolishes workers' self-esteem. You would want to know that. The secretaries, support staff, and people who used to work at this place know how difficult this boss is to work for. Family members of current and past staff could tell you stories about this manager. People who are likely to spill the beans about the workplace are the ones who are not in the inner circle. Rather, they tend to be more loosely affiliated with the workplace. They are the spouses of the people who work for the difficult boss. They are the former workers who have left the company and no longer have allegiance there. They are the support staff who worked for that castle. When you tell people in the village that you are looking for places that are busy, active, growing, and *have a good reputation*, meaning places where people like to go to work, you are checking out the workplace culture. People with loose or weak affiliations are more likely to be frank about what they have heard about the workplace culture and about individuals at a particular workplace.

How to Move from Quest to Campaign in an Informal Interview

There is another way to shift gears from the quest to the campaign phase. The shift occurs in the informal or informational interview.

Perhaps you have talked with a close friend and discussed your prototype workplaces and the neighborhoods you are looking for, and that friend has suggested that you meet with a contact of his who is in one of the right neighborhoods and is a nice person. You e-mail the contact, introduce yourself, and briefly describe the information you are looking for. You ask if he would be willing to talk with you. He says yes. You then briefly speak over the phone, and you can tell by the voice that you have a knight or wizard. You confirm a lunch.

You are now in the role of investigative reporter and new friend. You learn about his career and why he did what he did. In the process, you also ask questions and learn about where he works. You have been doing your research about places of interest and have learned about the various castles with potential in the neighborhood you seek to join. This contact is working at a company you have already thought might have the potential to be a good fit for you. He describes what he does and says positive things about his company and confirms that they are busy. At that point a little voice in your head might be saying, "I wish I could work there."

If you are thinking that, then use the "magic words" to change the focus of the conversation from quest to campaign by asking about whether your skills might fit and whether it makes sense to talk with whoever is in charge of hiring. Shift the conversation's focus, and learn the name of the key keeper. You have opened up the possibility that you would be interested in a job at this workplace.

In the informational interview, the scent of "job" is in the air. You never have to say the word *job*, because the contact is aware of your ultimate agenda. The person you are talking with knows that your goal is to land a job at the right workplace and that you are on the hunt. Avoid insincerity. If you say you have one agenda (information) and you clearly have an ulterior motive (job), you may lose your connection's interest. Therefore, I recommend the following approaches for most people.

First, if you have set up an informational meeting, go into that meeting expecting only to learn more about the workplace, the neighborhood, the contact person, and the market in general. Rely on your contact as a career counselor and market advisor.

Then, if you are more excited about the workplace during the informational meeting, and you have learned that your background fits well, go ahead and speak up about your interest. Do not be afraid to move the discussion into the campaign phase. Hesitation on your part may be seen as a lack of interest.

Finally, if the workplace where this contact is employed is one that is on your list of possible target workplaces, you can talk about your interest in landing a job there earlier in the meeting. Move into the campaign phase when you learn that the workplace is busy, active, and growing. Use the magic words that shift the conversation from quest to campaign.

When Can You Move Immediately into the Campaign?

If you already know the type of workplace that matches your skill set and you have a neighborhood you are a part of or can tap into, you may be able to find out where the work is flowing within this circumscribed neighborhood by employing a rapid telephone or e-mail campaign for a relatively quick search.

You Know the Neighborhood Already

This story comes from my practice with attorneys, but can be useful for anyone trying to find opportunities.

A young lawyer had been working for a litigation firm for about three years, the last two working almost exclusively for a very difficult partner. This partner had a reputation for being extremely critical of his associates, many of whom left the firm vowing to leave the practice of law altogether because they were so demoralized. After a pretty good beginning with this partner, the associate ran afoul of him as everyone else had and was sentenced to outplacement. It was a blessing in disguise, since she had been hoping to find a way out of this difficult situation and wanted a different practice area niche, as well. As is true with many associates, she did not have the time to search while she worked at the firm as the right-hand for this demanding partner.

The associate liked litigation. She wanted to move to a different litigation firm where she could get a fresh start in a different practice area with a more compatible partner. She had a pretty good idea of the comparable firms in town and had friends who were associates at many of these firms. She also had a wizard relative who was a litigator and a group of supportive partners at her old firm who liked her and were ready to say good things about her.

This associate was able to conduct a very quick search in the neighborhood she was qualified for in which she already had some contacts.

She conducted her job quest in textbook fashion by taking the following steps:

1. She met with the wizards, including her relative and the supportive partners.
2. She described what she was looking for in very clear terms and told people her goal and problem.
3. She engaged in a telephone and e-mail campaign with her friends at comparable boutiques and asked for information about whether their firms were busy, growing, and good places to work.

4. She met in person with many of her knights and wizards, reinforcing their trust and friendship. Her contacts gave her new contacts at firms beyond her knowledge base. She met with them as well. During her search for a new job, she worked full time and even left town for a brief trial, but by the second month of her search, she knew where she was likely to be hired and engaged in a campaign to have her supporters endorse her to other key people at the firms where she was hoping to work.

5. She worked on her interview skills by doing a mock interview and thinking through her best answers and preparing the anecdotal evidence to support her statements about herself.

She was hired at a litigation firm in the practice area she had hoped to move into just two months and twenty days after she began her search.

You Tap into the Network of a Supportive Wizard

When I first came to Chicago after practicing as an assistant district attorney in Philadelphia for two years, I needed a part-time job to support myself while I studied for the Illinois bar exam. I tried to figure out where my skills would be useful in the Chicago market. At that point I had a master's degree in social work, a JD from Temple University, and two years of litigation practice as a prosecutor. I thought that maybe I would be especially helpful to a lawyer doing divorce law because of my background in both counseling and litigation.

I did not know any divorce lawyers in Chicago, though I had been interested in the practice area and enjoyed my matrimonial law class in law school. I had recently read a book written by a divorce lawyer who practiced in Chicago, so I called his office. I got past the secretary by telling her that I enjoyed reading Mr. X's book and that I was a Philadelphia lawyer who had recently moved to Chicago. That was all I needed to say to be able to talk directly to this lawyer.

I began by telling Mr. X how much I enjoyed his book and also told him about my situation saying that I hoped to find a part-time job in matrimonial law while studying for the bar exam. I gave him a thumbnail sketch of my skills, said good things about myself by paraphrasing others, and explained why I wanted to find a part-time job doing matrimonial law. I said I didn't know if he had a need for someone with my background, but if he didn't, could he think of anyone else practicing matrimonial law who might need some extra help?

He told me he didn't need any help, but there were a few guys in town he could name who might like to have some assistance on a part-time basis. He began to list them and gave me some inside information about a number of them: this one was a barracuda and that one was expanding his firm and that other one was really a great guy but had gotten too busy and he could really use a hand whether he thought so or not.

What was surprising to me was his willingness to reveal so much about people and firms without knowing me. As he spoke, I simply encouraged him to say more by expressing my interest and joining with him around his remarks. When he said, "I have no idea why this guy is so disorganized, but I think it's only going to get worse," I asked, "Really? Why is that?" And he replied, "Because next year he's supposed to be the head of the matrimonial law committee for the bar association, and I have no idea how he's going to get everything done!"

Some people call this schmoozing, or small talk. You draw people out and encourage them to say more. The more they say, the more you learn. The more you join with them, the more they develop a comfort level with you. An ability to create a comfort level with new people you encounter is the essence of effective relationship building.

After I was done talking with this gregarious and helpful lawyer, I had the names of about five other matrimonial lawyers who were friends of his that he insisted I call. I had learned useful gossip about each one of them. "Call them up and tell them I sent you. Now don't say I vouch for your work, of course, but tell them we talked over the phone and tell them what you are looking for. I'm sure you'll find a part-time job for the summer if you do this."

So, with his blessing, I began calling his friends in this neighborhood of matrimonial lawyers, and I was amazed that I was able to talk with most of them by using the first lawyer's name, as he had told me to do. I was very clear about the fact that he did not know my work, but I had various judges and supervisors in Philadelphia who would be happy to recommend me. From the lawyers I talked with, I got the names of other lawyers to connect up with. I called about twenty lawyers in two days and got to talk with about a dozen of them. In each case, they were friendly and helpful and educated me about this realm of matrimonial lawyers, giving me more names of lawyers who might need help along with a brief description of each person. In each case, they were willing to gossip with me once they knew who had advised me to call.

By the second day, I had learned from more than one source about a lawyer who was generally described as a great guy who was overworked who needed help because his practice was so successful. When I called him up on the second day of my search, I mentioned that I had heard about him from other lawyers, who I named, and that all of them said I should call because he was so busy and maybe he could use some extra help for the summer. He laughed and said, "Why don't you come down to my office tomorrow? Maybe with your counseling background you can tell me why so many of my clients act as crazy as they do."

I met with him the next day, and we put together a part-time job to meet his needs and my needs. He was a truly wonderful guy, just as the other lawyers described.

Why did this search take only three days? Because I was invited to piggyback on the network of a wizard who was well-connected in the neighborhood and willing to allow me to use those connections. He was not only nice enough to share his network with me, he taught me a lot about how good networking is accomplished. Later, when I called him back to thank him, he told me that helping me to get introduced to the lawyers in his practice area was also a favor he did for his friends in the field. "And when you do a good job," he said, "that guy's going to thank me for helping him out." What goes around comes around.

Today this search might have to be a combined telephone and e-mail search. I would have tried to connect by phone, but if that did not work, I would have used e-mail, always mentioning the trusted contact in the subject line and the first line of the body of the letter. I would have asked this helpful wizard if he would be willing to send a brief e-mail to the people he recommended to me anticipating that I would be contacting them, so that my e-mail would not get sent to the spam filter. I would have tried to move from e-mail to phone to in-person meeting.

How to Campaign for a Job You Create

There are times when it is possible to actually create a position where there was no previous job at that workplace. The job is created because the work is there and your skill set matches the needs of the workplace. It also helps if one or two of the people who would endorse you already work there or are known to people who work there. You may need to produce a proposal to help key keepers and others feel comfortable with the decision to create a new position and then to hire you to do it.

A client I worked with a few years ago was a partner at a midsized firm and did work for a growing not-for-profit. As the not-for-profit grew, so did the complexity of its legal issues. This partner continued to handle most of the work, relying on others in the firm to address areas of law that were not his practice area. As time went on, this partner came to me for advice about how to wind down his career. He was ready to move out of the firm and did not need to make the same amount of money anymore, but he did not want to leave the practice of law altogether. He wanted to find work that was more meaningful to him, where, he said, "I can really feel good about the mission."

After some discussion, we agreed that he should try to convince the not-for-profit that trusted him already to consider bringing him in-house. He could save them money, and he already had a strong relationship with the key keeper and other insiders. He put together a proposal to show the board how he could help them trim their budget by bringing him in-house. He understood the company's history, their problems, and their legal needs. He also understood how law firms work and could oversee pricing and litigation done by outside counsel. He was the ideal candidate for this yet-to-be-created position.

The not-for-profit considered his request for a "to-be-created" job. The request was championed by the head of the not-for-profit, which made it more likely to be successful. Before hiring him, they advertised the position on their website, but this job listing was not really a viable position. The ad was a necessary step to satisfy protocol, but the job was already essentially taken by an insider – my client – who had created the position and led a successful campaign to land it.

There may also be an opportunity to create a job by approaching a workplace with a creative proposal or ideas that will help the company be more successful. This can be effective in a business context. If you take the time to study the company and approach the business entity with a good or creative idea, be sure you take steps to protect your creative effort, with a copyright, for example, before sharing it with the potential employer.

Part IV

Concepts to Utilize as You Work your Quest

Where you learn the four overarching concepts of the job quest, recognize the common pitfalls and how to avoid them, examine a model quest, and review concluding remarks.

Chapter Twelve:
Four Overarching Concepts

You are finding your way through the forest, talking with people, learning from them, and meeting new people with their assistance. You are figuring out how to get to the right castles. In the process you are already having interviews and giving back to helpful people. As you conduct your search, there are four valuable overarching concepts you can use in your efforts to find the realm and the job you seek.

- *One: More Magic Happens in Person*
- *Two: Trust Transfers*
- *Three: You Can Open the Treasure Chest with Your Dream and Dilemma*
- *Four: "Opportunism" Creates More Luck*

Let's talk about what these concepts are all about and how to use them to further your goals.

One: More Magic Happens in Person

WHEN PEOPLE MEET with you in person, there is greater potential for opportunity. Just the fact that you can experience, observe, and react to the body language is important. Subtle information is conveyed through gesture and nuance: the way she rolled her eyes when she said everyone is happy at that workplace; the way he hesitated just slightly when he said he had heard about a group breaking off from that large company to form a new company; the glance at a watch that tells you he is suddenly in a hurry. There are important pieces of information that are not conveyed unless you see and experience them in person.

Networking Using Golf to Make It Happen in Person

One of my clients, a litigation partner at a midsized firm, wanted to move to Florida to be closer to his wife's family after the birth of their children. He also wanted to change his career direction. He no longer wanted to be a lawyer. He wanted to move into a business role. He hoped to obtain an administrative position at a bank or hospital, but he had no direct experience in either realm. The only thing he had managed in his career was litigation.

He began his search for a job by contacting recruiters, but they were not responsive to his inquiries because he was trying to alter the kind of work he would be doing. He did not fit within the parameters of the searches most executive or legal recruiters handle. Recruiters he spoke with suggested that he not try for too much, that he should move to Florida but continue to be a litigator. But when he tried to contact law firms in Florida, they wanted to know if he had portable practice, namely, business clients he could bring with him, who would become clients of their firm. He did not have clients who would do that. He tried sending résumés and cover letters to companies he thought might be interested in him, making the case that his litigation background had enhanced his management skills and prepared him for a management position at a hospital or bank. He had no luck with that approach either. Most of the companies to which he sent résumés and cover letters responded summarily with rejections, saying that they were not hiring.

When we began working together, he was discouraged about his prospects for making this move. I also wondered if he was trying for too much. Moving to a new city and finding a job doing the same kind of work can be challenging enough. Relocating and changing career direction might be too hard to accomplish. Nonetheless, I gave him the job search training session, and then we brainstormed together. Did he have any gatekeepers, key keepers, or wizards who might help him out?

Did he know anyone who might help him meet with this group of people in the location in Florida he was trying to move to?

After some thought, he told me he probably had a pretty good wizard. His father-in-law had been the head of a small company in the Florida town where he and his wife hoped to move. Although the father-in-law's business was not very large, it was successful and well run. His father-in-law had made many friends in the business community, especially with people in the banking industry. He was a joiner. He had been a pillar of the business community in that town, contributing to local causes and supporting charitable events. He was well-liked. He had recently retired but still knew many people in that town. He was also eager to have his daughter and grandchildren move to Florida and live nearby.

So we put together a plan for my client to spend two long weekends in Florida playing golf. He contacted his father-in-law, and asked him to set up a series of golf outings with people who were part of the hierarchy at some of the good local banks and who might be interested in talking with him if he came to their attention through a trusted contact, namely, his father-in-law. They agreed that if nothing developed from their networking efforts, at least they would have some fun on the golf course together.

The next time I met with my client was after the arranged golf outings. He was meeting with me to do a mock interview session in preparation for a series of interviews for a management position with one of the banks he had been hoping would vet him for a job. The golf outings had done the trick. He landed interviews at some of the very banks that had originally sent him letters telling him that they were not hiring. He was able to accomplish the move to Florida and shift his career at the same time.

The relationship with his father-in-law helped him meet the key keepers and gatekeepers at some local banks. His interview helped him seal the deal. Could he have accomplished the same result without his father-in-law's help? He might have found friends or past colleagues who were living in Florida or who knew people in Florida in the banking world. He might have moved to Florida, found a non-associate role at a litigation firm by networking, developed relationships with the people in banks that he hoped would eventually consider him for a management job, created a positive buzz for himself in the local community, and possibly moved from there into the banking world on the business side. He might have found an opportunity in-house as a lawyer at a smaller bank and moved from there to the business side of the bank. All of this is speculation, but it is not fantasy because this is the way many people develop their careers. It can take time and effort, but it can also happen quickly with good relationship building. In short, good networking should include crafting or engineering meetings with key people who then help you advance your search. Ideally, you start with people who know and like you already to locate the people who could advance your cause and move you closer to the group of castles you would like to connect with. You might think that these people are only tangentially connected to the industry or market you are trying to enter, but you never know how helpful they might be until you interact with them. My client tapped into his wizard father-in-law's network to set up informal meetings that moved him closer to the formal vetting process.

In-Person Magic

Another example of this concept comes from my own background. When I graduated from law school, I applied to the district attorney's office in Philadelphia. I had been a social worker before going to law school, but I went to law school expressly to become a prosecutor. It was my dream job. So, after applying to the D.A.'s office, I waited, and heard nothing. Meanwhile, some of my friends from law school not only got interviews, but job offers. I asked my friends how they had been able to get an interview. All of them told me that they had a connection of some kind. Their dad knew the head of special prosecutions, or their brother was a cop and had a connection. I was shocked. Was that what it took to land a job at the district attorney's office? My friends looked at me with pity, I think. That was the way people got jobs out there in the real world. How was I so naïve?

At the time there was a Democratic primary campaign going on, and the district attorney race was very competitive. The Democratic incumbent was Emmett Fitzpatrick, and his primary challenger was Ed Rendell. This was Rendell's first attempt at political office. He eventually became the Governor of Pennsylvania, but this election was his first foray into political life. I liked what I heard Rendell talking about on TV and the radio. He was saying that he was not going to run the district attorney's office the way Fitzpatrick was doing it. Fitzpatrick's office was all about nepotism and cronyism, Rendell said, and he would change the hiring process to be a merit hiring system.

I perked up when I heard that. What if I could just get the chance to meet with him, even for a few minutes? I might be able to convince him that I would be a great hire for that office if he won the election. Maybe I was naïve. Maybe I was adventurous. Or maybe it was sheer desperation, but I was willing to think outside the box. If I had no chance to land the job of my dreams, then I had nothing to lose by pursuing it in an unorthodox way. I went to Rendell's campaign headquarters in Center City, Philadelphia, with my résumé in hand and a hope that I could meet with him.

When I got to campaign headquarters, I did not find Mr. Rendell. I found his secretary who was kind of an ogre. I explained to her that I wanted to talk with Mr. Rendell for just a minute if I could. She was irritable: "Yeah. Everyone wants to talk with Mr. Rendell for just a minute. Have a seat. He'll be back sometime today but I have no idea when. You can sit there if you want to."

So I waited. But I didn't just sit there. I started a conversation with her. I asked her about her involvement with the campaign and what she thought of Rendell and how things were going for him. We talked about the photograph on her desk, which was a picture of her grandkids. We talked about their activities and some of those activities were ones I enjoyed too. After a while I offered to put stamps on the envelopes she was mailing out. In short, we spent about four hours chatting together and had a pretty good time.

Late in the afternoon Rendell came in surrounded by his entourage. His secretary called over to him, "Hey, Ed, I've been talking with this young lady this afternoon and I like her! She wants a job." She had become a trusted contact in the time we spent together. Rendell waved me into his office. I knew that I only had only a few minutes to make a case for myself, so I launched into it. "Mr. Rendell, I have just finished law school and my dream is to be a prosecutor. That was the reason I went to law school. I was a social worker before I went to law school, but I hope you won't hold that against me. I really want to work in juvenile court and I think I could really be good there. I have been trying to get an interview with Emmett Fitzpatrick's office and I can't get one. Everyone says that without a personal connection to someone in the district attorney's office I will never even get an interview, and I don't have a connection."

Rendell said, "I can tell you will make a good prosecutor, and I'm not going to run the office hiring based on favoritism, but I have no idea whether I will win this election. It's about a fifty/fifty shot right now. So, tell you what, you leave your résumé with me, and if I do happen to win, send me a letter reminding me about our conversation, and if I am the next district attorney, you will have the chance to interview for a job." I was amazed and thrilled to hear him say this. I left his campaign headquarters thinking that I might actually have a chance to land this job after all.

Ed Rendell won the primary and then the general election, becoming district attorney. After he won, I sent him a letter reminding him of our conversation. I had an interview and landed my first job as a lawyer. I am certain that if I had simply sent my résumé to Rendell, it would not have been the same result.

One of the important lessons I learned about relationship building from this experience is that the trusted contact does not have to be a lifelong friend. I was open to talking with his ogre-like secretary, who proved to be a wizard and a gatekeeper for the castle and who endorsed me by saying she liked me. I also did some other good things that created luck.

First, I thought outside the box by deciding to show up at campaign headquarters with my résumé (Optimism/Opportunism). I was hoping to meet in person with Mr. Rendell (Interaction). I knew that the state's attorney's office routinely hired from a pool of new graduates, including graduates of my law school, so I should be part of a group of potential applicants the office would vet (Pragmatism). When I arrived at campaign headquarters, I found Mr. Rendell's secretary, and even though she was not initially very friendly, I had a hunch that we might hit it off (Intuition). I stayed for four hours waiting to meet for just a few minutes with Mr. Rendell (Tenacity). When we met, I advocated for myself and it worked out for the best (Opportunism).

I learned that more magic happens in person but there was another key lesson I learned also: Trust transfers. Trust transfers from the wizard or knight to you if the wizard or knight hits it off with you.

Two: Trust Transfers

The way trust transfers from a wizard or a knight to a job seeker has to do with the willingness of the contact person to vouch for you and also the depth of knowledge that this person has about you. A robust endorsement can come from someone you have just met who likes you, just as Rendell's secretary endorsed me after we had talked together. And if the wizard knows you, likes you, and knows your work and work ethic, that depth of knowledge can result in an even better endorsement.

Here is an illustration. Jan graduated from Sarah Lawrence College unsure about the career path she wanted to take. She was considering a career in teaching and thought about getting a master's degree in early childhood education, but wanted to have a job first as a teacher working with young children. She also had a strong interest in Japanese and had studied the language and the culture. She was thinking about a career involving something having to do with the Japanese culture as well. The job she wanted to find was one in early childhood working with Japanese children near enough to Manhattan that she could take a train to work. She researched bilingual Japanese/American preschools in and near Manhattan. The list of possibilities was very small.

There were a handful of nursery schools catering to the children of Japanese businessmen who were living in the United States and working in Manhattan. She decided these were going to be her target castles.

Jan started her campaign to be hired by contacting the school directors using a cover letter and résumé approach that she e-mailed to them. She only got one response. It was a rejection. It was a nursery school in Greenwich and it had been the one she had been hoping would hire her because she had heard about the school from one of her professors who knew the head of the school and it had sounded like the perfect place.

Jan talked with her professor about the school and asked if her professor would help her connect up with the director. Because she had been a very engaged student, her professor was happy to do that for her. She contacted the head of the nursery school and said good things about Jan. Trust transferred and Jan heard from the head of the school that she could come and visit, but the director cautioned that they had no jobs. Jan agreed to come for a visit just to observe the school.

Jan went for a visit. The director invited her to see the classes and also spend some time with the children reading to them at story time. Jan was able to converse in Japanese and made a good connection with the children, who liked her very much. At the end of the visit to the school, the director had Jan come into her office and asked whether she would be interested in taking a job with them as their creative arts teacher. This was exactly what Jan had been hoping for.

If Jan had not engaged the help of her wizard/professor, she would not have gotten in the door of the school. Once she had the opportunity to show up in person, more magic happened.

Three: The Treasure Chest and How to Open It

Another very valuable concept to use in your search is the idea that people can be treasure chests. By that, I mean that they may contain helpful connections and information that you would not know unless you are open to the opportunity to talk with them.

There is hidden treasure in the world. That treasure might be on the bottom of the sea near a wrecked Spanish galleon or on a deserted island that pirates frequent. If you are a treasure seeker, you dive down and search for the treasure chests that haven't been opened. You cannot know what is inside until you open them. There could be Spanish doubloons, golden goblets, or coins in the box. On the other hand, there might be nothing but dead fish and sand in there. The only way to find out what is inside is to open the box.

People can be amazing treasure chests; their treasure is their connections and information. Every person you meet is an unopened box of possibility, a potential treasure chest. You do not know what vital information a person holds unless and until you open the treasure chest. How do you do that? By telling people your dream and dilemma.

Think: You Never Know . . .

The treasure chest concept resulted from my observations of job seekers over many years. Some job seekers had preconceived expectations about who would be helpful to them and who would not. Many networkers thought this way:

> "If the person I am going to contact does not have a clear connection to a possible job, then it's not worth my time to try to meet up."

The default position for many networking job seekers seemed to be a belief that a contact person must be directly linked to a potential job to be worth the effort to connect and meet in person.

I also saw that many of the lucky networkers were finding out that contact people they did not expect to be very helpful were, in fact, giving them important leads and good information, and sometimes were even joining their round table and contributing advice and guidance. Often the first person in a line of linked contacts would not provide the job search treasure, but if the networker persevered and continued to network from contact to contact to contact, going beyond her closer friends into the realm of strangers, she would eventually hear of the opportunity that would provide that one job she needed, or link her to the very person she was trying to connect up with to get closer to the castle.

This makes sense when you realize that every person you know knows at least 100 other people, with a greater density of people he is interacting with in the field he is in. When you first start your quest, you are tapping into another person's knowledge and contact base, but that person usually does not have contacts that reach into every corner of the neighborhood. You are often starting with someone who is peripheral to the neighborhood or just tangentially connected to it. Many people do not know about activity across the entire realm of your industry, unless it is a very small community. For this reason, you need to move further into the neighborhood you are targeting and tap into other subgroups of connections to gain knowledge. As you progress, you get a fuller picture across the spectrum of your targeted neighborhood. You learn more about key people and which workplaces are busy and have good reputations. You also grow your relationships as you go.

If you consciously search for the very active, engaged, well-connected people (think of them as super-wizards), your chances or likelihood of connecting up with other people in the castles you want to reach can go way up. The super-wizards are very engaged people who connect with others and contribute to whatever field they are in. They often know more people and have created greater trust and connectivity in their neighborhood or realm. If you meet with them and they are impressed with you or even if they just like you, they have the potential to open up their rolodex or contact lists and offer you treasure.

Open Up the Box by Discovering Connections

Networkers who push beyond their close friends, into the realm of the knights and wizards – those strangers who are natural counselors and willing to be helpful – frequently report surprising coincidences, such as the discovery of common friends and similar strong interests with these new contacts. They are delighted to learn that they or their close family members have attended the same schools or colleges, or lived in the same cities or neighborhoods at one time in their lives, and may have enjoyed going to the same restaurants or have had similar experiences growing up. They may like the same music, share the same politics, have children with similar issues, and much more. These discovered connections are not only fun, they are also wonderfully helpful. Both the job seeker and newly discovered friend often feel closer as a result of finding a surprising connection or commonality. That new friend is usually more engaged and invested in the job seeker's quest in ways that would not have happened without that sense of affiliation and connectivity.

Job seekers usually attribute these surprising connections to luck, but once you are aware of the treasure chest concept and consciously apply it, it can be a valuable networking tool. These discovered connections are common and remarkably helpful for any job seeker. When job seekers uncover their shared interpersonal connections with other people, it helps create greater affiliation, attachment, and engagement. But the connection to the other person needs to be genuine and mutual, not merely self-serving. People are good judges of credibility. People know when you are sincerely friendly and caring or out for your own personal gain.

Open the Box by Talking about Your Dream and Dilemma

When you meet with people who are in a position to directly help you fulfill your job quest, you want to be sure you give them the right information and the best guidance so they can maximize their ability to assist you. You have done a great deal of work to prepare for this and other meetings with knights and wizards. You have figured out what you want in a job and the type of place you would like to work; you have studied where the workflow seems to be and begun to learn about the castles and the people in the neighborhood that you hope to join. You have prepared for your interview. When you happen upon a person who yields a treasure, you want to be ready to guide that person to advance your quest. You must also be ready to advocate for yourself. Part of that advocacy is revealing your dream and your dilemma to this well-positioned person.

Why use the words dream and dilemma? Because when you tell helpful people your dream and your problem fulfilling it, it motivates them to help you. When you share that information with others who are primed to help you, they care more and do more to assist your job search. If using the words *dream* and *dilemma* sounds too corny or dramatic, then use the words *goal* and *problem*, or *objective* and *difficulty*. Any of these pairings is effective.

When you share your dream, goal, or objective, and you use clear prototypes and enough detail to create an image, you help your contact not only identify places and people who could advance your search, but also identify personally with your vision. If you say you have a dream of being a project coordinator for a not-for-profit that helps kids be all that they can be, you are revealing your aspirations. You have already vetted this person and determined that she is a knight or wizard, someone who likes to help others. When you create an image of your aspirations, a knight, wizard or gatekeeper is likely to join you and try to assist you. The Make-a-Wish Foundation works on this principle. People who like to help others enjoy helping others realize their dreams, goals, or objectives. It feels good. It is empathically gratifying for them. But it only feels good if they also like you and experience a sense of connection with you.

When you share your dilemma, you are revealing the barrier to your success. For example:

> "I am hoping to be a videographer for a magazine that is developing a web presence and needs short pieces for the online readers. I could do those video stories. Can you think of a magazine that might be about to launch a website? I do not know of any but there must be some in need of this kind of help. Can you think of anyone in the industry who might have information about magazines that are starting an online presence?"

When you create a clear problem that needs to be solved, you are presenting your contact person with an opportunity to do something concrete to help you achieve your dream, vision, and goal. You have chosen to talk with this person because you have some reason to believe he could be connected to this realm. You are giving a person who likes to help others solve problems a chance to help you solve your problem.

The Treasure Chest Concept in Action

A good illustration of the treasure chest concept comes from my own experience after graduating from law school. As I mentioned earlier, I had gone to law school with the hope of becoming a prosecutor after graduation. After talking with classmates I learned that connections were the way to land an interview, and after going to Rendell's campaign headquarters, I learned that meeting in person could really help. Since I wasn't sure who would win the election, I needed to get contacts with both Rendell and the current district attorney, Emmett Fitzpatrick. How could I meet in person with Emmett Fitzpatrick or someone high up in that office?

I tried to think of anyone I knew who was even tangentially connected with the current district attorney's office. A friend came to mind. I had worked with her at a social service agency before going to law school. I had also heard that her husband was a lawyer and was politically active in the Democratic Party. I met John only briefly a few years before at a party. At the party, I overheard him talking with other people, and once or twice I heard him say "Emmett."

Emmett is a pretty unusual name. And I wondered if the Emmett he was talking about might be the district attorney. If he was on a first name basis with Emmett, didn't he have to be a close friend? I didn't know for sure. This was a hunch, but it was all I had.

I called Ginny and invited her and John to join me for dinner. I also mentioned that I would like to talk with John about what he knew about government jobs in Philadelphia and asked if that would be okay. She was very open to that idea and said John would be happy to help me.

They accepted my invitation and came for dinner. We had a good time. They talked about their children, and we told funny stories about our house renovation. We shared vacation stories and had a fun evening together. Finally we got to dessert. I gathered my courage and said, "Before you go, John, I have to ask you about something. I don't know how to say this, so I'm just going to put it out there. I have a dream and a dilemma, you could say. My dream is that I want to be a prosecutor, and my dilemma is that I have no personal connections with the district attorney's office. I hear I am not getting an interview there without a connection. Do you have any advice for me?" He said, "You do have a personal connection to that office. I'm the First Assistant District Attorney and our office is looking for more women to hire because it is embarrassing how few women we have working there. You'd be great, but do you really want that job?"

I was surprised to learn that I did have a connection at the district attorney's office and a pretty awesome one at that. I told John that becoming a prosecutor was the reason I had gone to law school, and I asked him if he would be willing to interview me. And he said, "Sure, let's do it right now. Why are you interested in being a district attorney? You social worker types are happier as public defenders, aren't you?!" I think he just wanted to mix it up with me to see how I would argue with him. That was my interview. It was about fifteen minutes long. After that he said, "Let's see how the election turns out. If we win, and you still want to work there, I will tell the guys I want you hired and you will be hired." I learned a lot from this experience. I pursued a meeting with John even though I did not expect it would be a direct link. If my friend's husband had turned out to have no connection with the district attorney's office,

I was ready to network from him to anyone he could introduce me to so that I could find my way to a gatekeeper for the district attorney's office. If he had not been able to help me, I would have followed other leads. I was determined to make that job happen.

The fact that this experience embodied a key concept for networking did not occur to me until I became a career counselor. For many years I thought I was just very lucky that my friend's husband turned out to be the first assistant district attorney. Over time, however, I saw this sort of story replicated with clients so often that I recognized a pattern. Job search luck improves if you take the approach that you cannot predict the outcome of a relationship or connection and you are willing to explore and invest in new relationships with an open mind.

Using the concepts I share with my clients and now in this book, I had engineered my luck. If Rendell won, I had a good chance to be hired, and if Fitzpatrick won, I had probably an equally good chance to be hired. As it turned out, Rendell won. I sent him a letter reminding him about our meeting at campaign headquarters, the interview was set up and it went well. I landed the job I had hoped to get.

As you conduct your quest, never assume that you know the extent of a contact's knowledge or contacts. Take the adventurous attitude that you never know what the next person you meet could help you accomplish; you never know who they could help you meet. When you discover new people, explore the curious and sometimes surprising affiliations that can bring you closer to people you thought were unconnected strangers. What you will learn is that these new people have many things in common with you that bring you closer. The discovery of new friends enriches your job search and your life in ways that are unpredictable but often remarkably helpful. You can open the treasure chest by telling people your dream, goal, or objective and your dilemma, problem, or difficulty.

Every person you meet on your quest could yield a hidden treasure.

In addition, there are times when you know you could get further in your quest if you could engineer a meeting with someone who is a gatekeeper or a key keeper for a particular workplace. That gets us to the fourth overarching concept: Opportunism Creates More Good Luck.

Four: Opportunism Creates More Luck

What is *opportunism?* When we talked about luck and how it gets created, there were four elements we added to Richard Wiseman's attitudes that generate more luck in life. One of the added elements is opportunism. Opportunism is the combination of an adventurous attitude and purposeful, creative engineering to get to meet up with people who are important for the success of your quest. It kind of feels like stalking, but not creepy stalking, rather it is actually research and inventive, clever strategy to move you toward your goal. This is what I have seen the gifted, natural networkers do. When these elements come together, it creates more opportunity for the job seeker. However, good, intuitive judgment also matters when a jobseeker pursues creative meet-ups.

Creating Opportunity at the Dog Park

One of my clients came to work with me to determine her career direction after leaving an in-house position. After doing the preliminary work to identify a good career direction, it was clear that she was a great match for management consulting for law firms. She was also a naturally good networker, and once she figured out the right career direction, she began the quest for information about where there might be a job in that very limited field in the city where she lived. She learned about a consulting job at a well-respected management consulting firm that had been vacated for more than a year. She learned that the job had not been filled. She set about trying to find a way to come to the attention of the workplace through a trusted contact.

My client knew of only one person in the field of management consulting for law firms, and he lived right down the street from her. She did not know him personally, but she knew what he looked like, that he had a dog, and that he took his dog to the same neighborhood dog park that she and her dog frequented. She had seen him walk his dog past her house before and had seen him at that dog park in the past. She decided to engineer a meeting with him at the dog park, so she could talk with him about management consulting and learn whatever gossip she could about the field. One morning she lay in wait, watching out her front window to see when he would walk by her house with his dog heading for the dog park. As soon as she saw him go by, she quickly got her dog on a leash and set off after him.

Once at the park, it was easy to meet him and start a conversation that led to a longer discussion. Through him, she learned more about the management consulting firms in town and was able to obtain information about the company with the vacancy. She contacted the consulting firm and confirmed that the spot was still not filled. After that, she launched an effective campaign to convince the firm to hire her for that open position, which they eventually did.

Finding creative ways to meet up with important gatekeepers can be a useful strategy, but it has to be done in a reasonable way. You need to keep your efforts to connect with people within acceptable, conventional bounds based on the particular workplace culture and the situation. That means that you need to ask the knights and wizards you talk with about how that workplace tends to find their hires. Do they use recruiters? Do they rely on ads? Would you be welcome if you showed up in person on the doorstep? Sometimes you have to rely on your intuitive judgment and be sensitive to the circumstances. My client who found a creative way to "bump into" the management consultant at the dog park did it in a clever and effective way. Appearing at this man's home or at the consulting firm without any introduction would have been too unconventional and possibly damaging. She also impressed this consultant enough to meet with her more extensively.

A Creative Way to Meet Up with a Gatekeeper

Later in my career, after I had been working as a prosecutor in state court, I wanted to try to be hired by the U.S. attorney's office in Chicago, and I relied on some of these same concepts again. By this time, I had been an assistant state's attorney for about three years in Philadelphia and then in Chicago at the state's attorney's office in Cook County. I had gained experience doing hundreds of trials in state court and had overseen investigations in the official misconduct unit, which is the state court skill set that is similar to the kinds of investigations and trials done by the U.S. attorney's office. I had applied to become a federal prosecutor, but my application seemed to be bogged down.

I was waiting to hear from the office to arrange an interview, but months went by without an interview. I knew that people with my experience in state court were hired by the U.S. attorney's office, but that there were hundreds of applicants for a small number of positions. I decided to try to find a wizard to support my efforts.

I learned that one of the key people who served as a gatekeeper for the U.S. attorney's office was Senator Chuck Percy of Illinois. What I heard was that if you had the right credentials, the senator could get you a close look or a second look by the U.S. attorney's office. I set out to try to meet with Senator Percy. I started my quest by asking my friends on the north shore if they knew anyone in their father or mother's age group who knew Chuck Percy or had gone to school with him. Percy grew up in Kenilworth, north of Chicago, and I had been raised in a nearby suburb. Many of my friends' parents were the right age to have been in school with Percy. I found out that one of my close friend's dad had been a good friend of Percy's and still had a relationship with him. I asked my friend if I could meet with his dad. And that was arranged. I brought my résumé to the meeting and explained why I had the skills and background to be a terrific assistant U.S. attorney and why it would be wonderful if I could meet with Senator Percy. My friend's dad said he would pass along my information to Percy. But that never happened. Time went by, and each time I checked, my friend's dad had not done that introduction yet but promised he would. Months went by, and I decided that I needed to be more creative about meeting the senator.

By talking with people and hearing more about the senator, I learned that Senator Percy was a tennis player, and that he played at the same courts where I played. I made it a point to find out when he would be there and arranged to play on the same court after he finished. As he left the court I went up to the senator, shook his hand and said, "Senator Percy, it's a pleasure to finally meet you. I've almost met you for the past four months." I explained that I had met with his friend, that I had been hoping to get an introduction to talk about why I would make a terrific assistant U.S. attorney, and that I had the right background for the job. After talking with me briefly, the senator agreed to meet with me for an informal interview and asked me to bring my résumé. We talked for about twenty minutes, and I left my résumé with him. Almost immediately after that I received a letter inviting me to call to arrange an interview at the U.S. attorney's office. The interview went well, and I was hired as an assistant U.S. attorney.

Showing Up in Person without a Knight or Wizard to Introduce You

When I work with clients, I do not routinely encourage them to just show up on the doorstep of the workplace where they want to be hired. Despite that general advice, I have had a number of clients who are very engaging people and are naturally comfortable with adventurous situations. Some of them have successfully used this tactic to land jobs in workplaces that turned out to be open to such an approach.

One woman I worked with was trying to move from the practice of law to a related but non-legal field involving work-life balance issues. She had gotten involved in activities supporting work-life balance in the law and saw an advertisement for a position for a sales and marketing position at a workplace she had heard good things about. She had actually kept clippings of articles about this workplace and their activities for many years because she was excited about what they were doing. Armed with her convincingly yellowed newspaper articles in her file folder and her résumé, which she revised to highlight the background that fit with the position she sought, she showed up at the doorstep of that company and asked if she could speak to the person in charge of hiring.

In the informal interview that followed, she talked about her longstanding interest in the employer's mission and showed that person the file of articles she had kept. Even though other applicants might have had more appropriate skill sets, she landed that job. The reason her approach was effective was particularly because of the small size of the workplace (approximately 15 employees), her positive and assertive, but not aggressive approach, and her evidence of prior longstanding interest in, engagement with, and knowledge of the field and knowledge of their specific company.

Many gifted networkers land jobs by employing creative networking approaches, such as engineered meetings. However, creative networking requires good judgment, planning, sensitivity, people skills, and some courage to think and act outside the box while exercising caution about conforming to workplace expectations and norms.

A Tale of Two Creative Networking Attempts

Sometimes, despite your best effort to create a meeting, it does not have the desired result. One woman I worked with many years ago went to a fundraiser for the incumbent state's attorney hoping to meet with him there and express her interest in working at that office. There were many other people at the fundraiser that night, and some of these people held more interest for the incumbent. She might have done better to volunteer at that state's attorney's office or land an externship and do outstanding work that would gain her recognition with people in the office who would then endorse her for a job as an assistant state's attorney.

She might have had a different experience at the fundraiser if she had networked more and found an endorser who also could connect her to either the state's attorney himself or to someone known and trusted by him. If that person had introduced her to the incumbent, she might have had better luck.

On the other hand, another client created her own luck at a fundraiser by finding a way to meet with the manager of a company she had hoped would interview her. She had seen the manager's name as a speaker at a fundraiser for a cause she had long been involved with, so she made sure to attend. After he spoke, she introduced herself and talked with him about their shared interest in this not-for-profit. Then she expressed her honest, long-standing interest in his company. He asked her to come by for an interview, and although it took a few months for the business to develop a need for a new hire at her level, she was hired by the firm about six months later.

Do Your Homework and Get Creative

Finally, another fun illustration of opportunism comes from a young woman, Chris, who wrote articles for a magazine. She learned about a job at a fashion magazine and was able to set up an interview. Then she searched the Internet to find out more about the interviewer's strong interests. Chris learned that this woman had a favorite designer. Chris also liked that designer and had recently bought a scarf by him. When Chris went for the interview she was wearing a simple outfit and that designer's scarf. When she met the interviewer they started off their conversation talking about the scarf and the designer they both liked so much. She got the job.

Opportunism is really nothing more than persistent research with a purpose and goal to find a way to meet up with the individual you think could advance your search.

Chapter Thirteen: Common Pitfalls and How to Avoid Them

When I teach this quest-to-campaign rapid relationship approach to clients and send them out to conduct their searches, I set up another session after a few weeks to see how they are doing. Some of my clients come to the session beaming. They have uncovered a number of good opportunities or are hearing about some places with potential. Some of them are into the interview phase or are deciding between a few job options. But not everyone has an easy time of it. Here are some of the common pitfalls that job seekers may encounter.

Failing to Direct and Guide Your Knights and Wizards

THE SINGLE BIGGEST PROBLEM I hear about when clients return to describe their quest status is a failure to work closely with the knights and wizards and guide them to provide the needed search information. Many of the well-meaning people you meet with as you conduct your quest have been asked to give other people help in their job searches. And those other people have asked for advice and information about where the jobs are. You can't blame your contacts for thinking that that is the information you want also.

Unless you guide your natural counselors with clear messaging and requests, you run the risk that these people will fall back into job-finder mode and try to provide you with overly brief information about jobs, not where the work is flowing, not descriptions of workplaces that fit your needs, or other on-the-ground information you are looking for. It is up to you to patiently go back and describe again the information you seek.

Another potential hazard in the quest process is failing to keep the focus on your core message. You want to walk the contact person through descriptions of the workplaces you seek. People I work with will often identify two or three types of workplaces or two or three possible career paths that would be good matches. Guiding your natural counselors works best if you clearly identify each option and actually label the options when you talk about them. You can say you want to describe these options separately and then do that. Then clearly describe option one, option two, and option three with your contact, detailing the key aspects of each one by one, and then ask your contact to identify the helpful people in the castles and the related realm.

You have to do this because of the treasure chest concept – you never know who your contact knows – even if you might think that you do. Your contact could be your professor and you might think she would probably know people in academia, but she could turn out to have a sister, friend, or spouse who is working in a totally unrelated field that you are interested in learning more about. You never know. Your contact working in a traditional institutional setting could be married to someone who created a successful start-up company and could use some help from a person with your skill set. You never know. You have to open each box one at a time to get the fullest benefit from your conversation with the knight or wizard.

Failing to Provide Clear Prototypes

All too often the job seeker is either not clear enough or too detailed about describing the opportunity sought. Lack of clarity can confuse a contact person who is trying to help by suggesting places that fit the description the job seeker is giving. Be clear enough to prompt an idea of workplaces that match the descriptions in the minds of your contacts without ruling out too many potentially good workplaces. If the description is overly detailed, the person may not be able to imagine another place that is similar.

An example of how this relates to job search comes from a client of mine who wanted to do criminal defense work at a law firm. He had been at a large firm, so as he conducted his networking, he described only large workplaces to his contact people. He failed to include specialized smaller shops, called boutiques, in his descriptions, so his contacts did not recommend any smaller firms, even though some boutiques might have been a very good match for his needs. By being too narrow about the size of the workplace, he may have lost out on opportunities that might have been right for him.

Another client was overly narrow in his description of what he wanted to find. He said he would like a job in a corporation overseeing product liability litigation. But his background in litigation made him a good candidate for many other opportunities. He ended up in a government job with the postal service, but his search took longer than he had hoped, possibly because he started out with an overly narrow focus.

Failing to Move Beyond Biography

Another common mistake job seekers can make is to be stuck in the role of biographer when talking with their knights and wizards. Often these networkers understand that networking is about friendship and they take that to heart, but they engage the contact person in a long conversation about his or her career that does not advance beyond the contact person's own biography.

This is appropriate when the networking is purely informational and the goal is to find a better fitting career direction and hear about the new field. But for a job quest, which is more focused, the information you need goes beyond your contact's biography. It is very important to obtain market knowledge and learn the gossip, as well as convey clear information about the kinds of workplaces you are trying to find out about. You need to guide your contact to the topics you want to learn about and ask for advice, information, market knowledge, the names of more knights and wizards, and whether you can get your contact to open the door with these additional contact people. You also want to ask whether this contact person would be willing to send an e-mail explaining why you are going to be following up with an e-mail or a phone call to those additional people. You want to get that e-mail introduction to ensure you do not end up in the spam filter.

Using the "J" Word Too Soon

We have seen that the mention of the word *job* early in your networking can have a chilling effect and might limit your luck. Although it is true that you are looking for a job, attempts to talk about jobs will often stunt the conversation and limit the knowledge you obtain. Instead of using the "J" word early in your networking efforts, focus instead on creating a viable trust relationship in which there is give and take. Ask for advice, information, and market knowledge. Engage your natural counselors in a discussion by using your core message and learn from them. Do not let others take the role of being your recruiter unless you have great faith that they will not drop the ball. Make the focus of your discussion the master list of people and places you have developed, the prototypes you have described, and your dream and dilemma. Be sure to also ask for ideas about more people and places to add to your growing list of wizards and knights.

Allowing an Ogre to Defeat You

Although most people are well-meaning and helpful, there are a handful of people you could encounter in your quest who are not. They may even start out seeming to be helpful people but at some point they change into ogres. They might tell you that your search is not going to be productive; they might give you bad advice; they might put you down in some way. If you encounter someone who puts a damper on your enthusiasm or who tells you that you have no chance to get a certain kind of job, take that opinion under advisement. Do your homework. Be sure your credentials are close enough to those of other people who already work there, for example. Understand the odds you face. But do not let an ogre defeat you.

Running Back to the Cottage to Send Résumés to Dragons

Quests are not easy; that's why they are heroic. They can be time consuming and require courage and energy, but the payoff is great. Not only do you land the job you know you want because you have defined what you are searching for, but you develop wonderful friends during your journey. Some of them will join your round table, and many will become your sources of business and life-long friends as your career moves forward. There are, however, some job seekers who venture into the forest briefly, encounter an ogre, and run back to the safety of their cottages, sending résumés to castles as their primary method of job search. There is nothing wrong with continuing to watch for jobs on the Internet that appear to be great matches for you, unless it becomes an overly time-consuming activity. There is nothing wrong with checking websites of the firms and companies that your research tells you would be great matches for you. There is nothing wrong with checking in from time to time with recruiters to see whether they will work with you based on any recent orders they have to fill. But if you do not try rapid relationship and trust building, you miss too much of the hidden job market, limit your effectiveness, and miss out on the long-term career benefits of meeting people in your professional neighborhood.

Failing to Explore Alternative Arrangements

There can be many reasons for a slow search. A poor or uncertain economy will yield fewer jobs simply because the work is not flowing well. Searches can take longer because employers are nervous about hiring anyone until they trust the sustainability of the workflow. In that case, the employer may hope to increase the productivity of the current staff and avoid new hiring as long as possible. In such instances, the potential employer may be more open to the idea of temporary assistance, independent contracting, or part-time help. These arrangements can be suggested by the job seeker and explored with the employer, because it is a way to get a foot in the door. And that can lead to a job.

To that end, failing to explore possible alternative arrangements with the potential employer is a common job search mistake. The job seeker thinks, "If I do not get the opportunity for a full-time job right away, I need to move along in my search." Very often, however, a professional who creates a relationship with a workplace by starting out in a role, such as an intern or apprentice or on a part-time basis may be able to add value to the workplace and evolve into a full-time job. The people who are most successful at making this shift to full-time generally try to create relationships with other key people at the workplace while doing outstanding work. Not all workplaces will be open to this shift from internship, apprenticeship, or part-time work to full-time job, but even if that is not in the cards, the job seeker is getting experience and additional skills, not to mention making some money.

Chapter Fourteen: A Model Quest

Let's demystify the secret of how luck can be created by deconstructing a model search to study the components of luck and chance and see how they combine with motivation and clear-eyed assessment to generate options for one job seeker.

At the beginning of the recession in 2009, I received a call from a law firm asking if I could work with a client in need of outplacement. She was a fourth-year associate in the estate planning group. I met with this lawyer a few days later and learned about her background.

Agnes was the first-born child of hard-working Russian immigrants who had come to the United States while she was in junior high school. She worked hard in high school and attended a good state university where she majored in economics and graduated with honors. After graduation she found a job as a financial advisor at an investment firm. At this firm she handled internal legal issues and compliance issues, counseling clients and working with in-house legal counsel. She enjoyed accommodating clients' needs and fielding financial questions. She felt most engaged when she helped clients one-on-one.

She kept that job for three years and then attended law school, where she graduated with honors and a 3.5/4.0 GPA. While in law school, she found her tax courses particularly interesting and went on to get an LL.M. in tax. She graduated with highest honors.

After graduation, she took a position with a well-respected, relatively large law firm. She stayed there for two years. However, the firm lost a key partner when he moved to a different firm and took his clients with him. Since Agnes's work as an associate depended on business from this partner, she was affected by the loss of the business he brought in. The firm referred her to me for outplacement.

When I first met with Agnes, she told me that she had already been actively trying to find a job for a few weeks. She was doing a combination of searching on the Internet and interacting with people in the neighborhoods she thought might turn out to be fruitful.

With my advice, Agnes figured out the key legal neighborhoods that might yield good results for her, given her skills and background. She developed knowledge about where the workflow would be likely, and where she could engage in client counseling, which was her strength. She correctly figured out that with the stock market falling dramatically, many people would be concerned about wealth management and would want to be certain about how to protect whatever assets they had, as well as protect their wealth for the next generation. She talked with people in wealth management to validate this idea. She learned that wealth management was a hot area, becoming hotter as a result of the collapse of the up side of the market.

Knowing this, she then looked at the types of workplaces that made the most sense for her and were likely to need help. She came up with three: banks, accounting firms, and boutique law firms with corporate and estate planning practices. Then she launched her job quest.

Agnes had been an outstanding associate at her firm, and many of the partners there were happy to assist her. She met with them and worked with them to identify people and places that fit the realms she thought would be good bets. These partners turned out to be very helpful and provided her with names of people for networking purposes as well as law firms that fit the description she gave them.

She also tried to work with recruiters, but very few recruiters were being asked to do associate searches because of the recession. She realized that she was on her own, but instead of getting depressed about that, she seemed to step up the pace of her networking interactions in an effort to learn more and work her search harder.

With my assistance, Agnes reworked her résumé and did a series of mock interviews to prepare for informal networking interviews.

She learned how to conduct a productive job search of rapid relationship and trust building. She already seemed to understand most of the concepts, but she told me that it was helpful to her to know that she was doing the right things in her search. No one had ever taught her to do this and she wasn't sure she was doing her networking the right way. She also changed some of her messaging, such as delaying the use of the "J" word until she had identified places she knew could be good prospects for her, engaging in longer in-person meetings with contact people, and using prototypes to help contacts identify good workplace prospects for her. She showed her contacts a partial master list of people doing the work she wanted to do, and places where her skill set would fit the needs of the workplace.

Agnes was fearless about finding knights and wizards. She considered ogres to be calculated nuisances. She was undaunted about meeting with anybody and everybody. She instinctively knew when to ask for the endorsement from supportive partners. Her search efforts also stood out because of the energy and positive mindset she brought to her search, as well as her willingness to try out new ideas.

Agnes learned of a smaller firm with the wealth management practice area she had figured out was going to grow, driven by client need. She approached the firm by asking a supportive partner who knew good people at that firm to open the door for her, which he did by sending an introductory e-mail. She was invited to meet with key partners for lunch, which turned out to be her informal interview. She continued her job search and uncovered an interesting prospect at a bank. She kept the law firm informed about her other job prospects, which probably made the firm nervous that they might lose her. They extended her an offer.

Almost exactly one month to the day after we met for the first session, Agnes landed the job she wanted at the boutique law firm she had targeted. She also uncovered three other excellent prospects that probably would have become job offers had she declined the offer from the law firm. No doubt, part of her success was due to the fact that the failure of the economy on the up side of the market generated workflow on the down side of the market in the form of asset protection for future generations, and Agnes had the skill set to help clients with that problem. She is also the kind of natural networker who lands on her feet.

Chapter Fifteen:
Concluding Remarks

We have come to the end of our journey together, and by now I hope you are more confident about what you need to do to have a productive job search. I hope you think of your job search as a quest. You are the hero, setting out into the forest to find your way to the castles that could be good for you, your search progressing from trusted contact to trusted contact.

I hope you have a positive attitude about how to think about your job search, and a host of ideas about how to proceed and how to make this quest productive, not only in helping you find a new job, but in helping you find your virtual round table – that group of people who will support you for your entire career. In addition, you can gain many professional connections that will not only open doors for you over time but enrich your life because you are now part of a community of people who enjoy interacting and participating in the same industry you are engaged in.

These ways of thinking add to your luck. Mindset and knowledge maximize good luck because you understand that what you might have thought of as a lucky or chance encounter has come from your efforts, your intuitive judgment, and your awareness of how the process of a job search works. As a result you can generate more so-called lucky encounters and results.

One of my clients had an experience that underscores this point. He had reached the point in our work where he had the job quest training session and had identified a number of companies that were good matches for his skill set and background and fit with his career goals. He brainstormed with me about how to connect with key people who could advance his quest. He mentioned that his local professional association was having a lunch meeting on a topic that was central to his industry, but one that he already knew a lot about. I pushed him to go to this meeting, even if the information he would learn there might not be so important for him. He hesitated, saying that he had a lot of work to do. But he did not rule it out.

When I met with him next he reported that he had gone to the meeting. "I took the attitude that you never know, you just never know what will happen. You will never guess who was sitting nearby!" he told me. "It was an old friend of mine. We got to talking and it turns out he is a good friend of one of the managers at one of the companies I told you about. He's going to help me out by introducing me to this guy. The three of us are going to lunch next week. I can't believe my luck!"

I agreed that this was a wonderful turn of events, but I didn't agree that it was just luck. He had set the stage for luck to happen for him. He had already identified the companies and people he wanted to connect with. He went to the meeting that he did not think would be helpful, but he took the approach that *you never know if there could be a treasure chest somewhere.* He talked with his friend in a way that elicited the information he needed. The fates did not conspire to cause this amazing result and it did not happen purely by chance. He created the potential for good fortune. Why not take some credit?

If job seekers are motivated, know what to do and how to do it, and persevere with a sense of undaunted purpose, humor, curiosity, and generosity, they make luck happen.

You can do this. You know what to do. You know how to prepare before you leave on your adventure: identify your career needs, find the workflow, redo your résumé, and do research about the castles. You are armed with your computer, so you can continue to do research as you find your way through the woods. You are ready to strike out on your journey, over the mountains and through the forest, where you will meet many engaging and interesting characters, knights and wizards who will help you and become your friends and guide you to find the gatekeepers and key keepers. You know how to help them in return. You know how to ask the right questions to find your way to the realms surrounding the castles. Outsmart the dragon at the drawbridge by taking the path to the side door or the back door, where you find the marketplace full of people who can teach you about the realm if you talk with them in a productive way. You know about ogres and how to keep them from stopping you. You know that you may have to fight the urge to retreat to the safety of your cottage.

When you have figured out the castles and know which ones may be able to use your help, you know you will need to launch your campaign to have your supportive wizards and knights speak up on your behalf and link you to the gatekeepers and key keepers in these castles. This is the time to use the word *job* and ask for endorsements. You can ace the interviews because you are prepared and you have recruited yourself to a workplace for which you are a good match.

This is your quest. You are in charge. You can do a lot to create *good luck!*

Appendices

Where you learn about the AIMS Assessment, the AILS Assessment, and the Essential Elements Assessment, learn how to build a skills-based résumé, see a Master List of People and Places, and review the key steps to execute in your successful job quest.

A Note on the Appendices

THE ASSESSMENT TOOLS in the first three appendices are the ones I use in my practice. When I counsel people, I start with the tools in the first two appendices, AIMS and AILS. With the AIMS assessment, if you have the aptitude and interest, and the market need is there but you are missing the skills, then all you need to do is acquire the skills and you are all set to launch the search. Or let's say you are dissatisfied with your career but are not sure why. You would try to identify what AILS you. For example, if you have the aptitude and interest for a job but are not happy with the lifestyle or the culture of the workplace, you could move to a different job in the same field. Sometimes, though, a deeper assessment is required to figure out the right career direction if you are just starting out or changing fields. Some people need to go on a journey before the job quest journey begins to figure out enough about who they are to know what kind of job to look for. This is where the Essential Elements exercise is valuable.

When I work with clients, much of our early work is devoted to this self-assessment. We try to figure out and identify the building blocks a person needs to be satisfied at work. We get at that by doing a work history and personal history. Once that work is done, we can put together an Essential Elements list, identifying those elements a person needs and those elements that really need to be avoided. Then we see how much each element matters and how much give there might be for every identified element. This exercise creates greater clarity about what each person must have in her career and what should be avoided. We can use this Essential Elements list to measure a job to understand what the job has and why it is or isn't a match. The list can also be used to determine good questions to ask in an informational interview to learn what is likely to be satisfying about a possible career or job as well as what is likely to be problematic.

For some, it will be helpful to do these exercises. For others, it might be insufficient. Trying to assess ourselves can be difficult. Sometimes we do not really know ourselves very well and tools like the ones in this book might be difficult to utilize. If these tools do not provide the information you need for an effective self-assessment, use your high school or university career services office to find out about tests that could help you learn more about yourself. Myers-Briggs is a favorite, but there are others, including Highlands Ability Battery, Strong Interest Inventory, and Johnson O'Connor. Some private career counselors and career services professionals at your school should be able to help you with this process of self-assessment as well.

NOTE: All these Appendices are also available as a PDF download from my website at http://www.nielsencareerconsulting.com/jobquest/.

Appendix A: AIMS Assessment

The AIMS assessment stands for Aptitude, Interest, Market Need, and Skills. You need to assess these four elements to point yourself in the right career direction.

WHO SHOULD DO the AIMS assessment?

You should do an AIMS assessment if one of these describes your situation:

- You are a new graduate and want to figure out the right career path.
- You are in a field or industry already but want to move to a different segment of your current field or industry.
- You are in a field or industry but want to move to a new field or industry and you are not sure what that should be.

1. Aptitudes

What do you do well?

Most people excel at work when they are performing work and activities that play to their strengths. For example, some people are naturally good at math or science, while others are not as good at thinking that way. Some people are excellent logical, linear thinkers. Some people write well. Some people are good at understanding how other people think and are sensitive to nuances in human behavior. *Aptitudes* are our innate strengths and abilities.

For a job to be satisfying and a career path to be highly successful for you, it helps if your work utilizes your strong suits. If you are innately good at what you do, you will be more likely to be satisfied and successful at work.

Think back over your life to identify your aptitudes. Include those identified by your teachers, friends, and family. Are you the person everyone talks to because you are easy to connect with? Are you the person who loves being in the center of a group? Do you enjoy the spotlight? Are you the person who wants to help others? Are you the person everyone knows will get the right answer on the history exam? Sometimes other people can see our personal strengths more clearly than we can, so ask friends, teachers, and family to add to this list if you need help.

APTITUDE WORK SHEET

What do you do well naturally? What are your talents and gifts? List them.

1. _____

2. _____

3. _____

4. _____

5. _____

6. _____

7. _____

8. _____

9. _____

10. _____

11. _____

12. _____

13. _____

14. _____

15. _____

APTITUDE WORK SHEET ILLUSTRATION

This person went to journalism school after college and earned a master's degree there. She became a freelance videographer and video content producer for a magazine developing a Web presence. The job requires excellent interpersonal skills meeting with vendors and learning about their businesses and then telling their stories in a compelling and upbeat way. The job requires motivation to create video content and an eye for detail. She likes to work independently and will make deadlines without being supervised.

1. Good at projects that require creativity and visual ability.
2. Good at talking with anyone about anything. Meets new people easily.
3. Loves putting music and visual content together.
4. Independent projects that require close attention to detail.
5. Good at helping people feel at ease, a good hostess.
6. Natural sense of humor.
7. Interested in popular culture and music.

2. Interests

Interests are not necessarily the same as aptitudes.

What is an interest? It's the thing that gets you out of bed in the morning. It's the motivator for your work-life. You really look forward to doing this activity or thinking about this topic. For some people, it's a passionate excitement about something. For others, it is a strong interest in something. And for others it's a sense of fulfillment or engagement that may not rise to a level of passion or even strong interest, but when doing the activity, the person enjoys life more.

To have a career that works, we want to have an interest in what we are engaged in doing on a daily basis. Certainly it is not possible for a job to be totally interesting all of the time. Most people understand that. But if there is a very low level of interest in any aspect of the work we do a lot, and there is nothing else in the work setting that captures our interest currently or has the prospect of future gratification, then the job will not be compelling. If the job is not compelling, you will have a hard time staying committed.

Interests can include such things as spending time with people we enjoy interacting with; learning how to be better at something we value; learning how to manage and execute a project; or contributing to a compelling cause that we believe in. For some, the work itself might not be interesting, but other factors could outweigh that fact. If the person enjoys the workplace culture and interactions with coworkers and clients and he can have a full life outside of work, that can create enough interest to maintain long-term motivation. In that situation, the lifestyle is the motivator.

In this exercise, try to list your strong interests. If you have an interest in having a life that includes many activities that you engage in outside of the workplace setting – training for a marathon, helping out at a shelter for battered women, learning karate, teaching Sunday school, traveling, writing fiction – list them as well. If you are strongly motivated to engage in activities outside of work, you will need to plan to have a job that allows you to have time for these activities.

Another way to figure out your interests is to imagine all of the blogs, books, and magazines in the world on a table in front of you. What would you pick to read about? Where do you spend your browsing time on the Internet? Do you read blogs? Which ones? What topics interest you? What do you gravitate toward?

There are many people whose strong interests shift as priorities change. Interests can change radically when a person has a change of status. Examples of a change of status include marriage, a child, or an illness of a loved one or oneself.

Finally, are you interested in the field? Do you like thinking about whatever it is the job will require you think about? If not, that is important. Many people go into a field for the wrong reasons. They are encouraged by friends and family. They want to make money. They do not know what else to do. It is remarkable to me as a career counselor how many people I have worked with who really do not like thinking about the concepts or the day-to-day content of the work they are doing. If you lack that basic interest that is a very important piece of information about yourself that probably should lead you to consider leaving the field for a career that does engage your interests, as long as your economic situation does not stop you from that move. You want to be aware of and "listen" to your interests to lead you into the right career.

An example of how to think about listening to your interests to lead you to the right career comes from one of my clients who got into the wrong industry after graduation. He entered the field of finance after majoring in political science and economics at a top tier university. Most of his friends chose finance, so he did too. He soon realized that he had no interest in the topics or the daily work of the job he did, and looking ahead, he had no interest in becoming an expert in the field he worked in. Interactions with coworkers were not gratifying enough to make up for the deficits of the career. His strong interests throughout his early life would have led him to think about becoming an engineer or an architect. He was the guy who made drawings and models of houses just for fun. He was the guy who took apart the alarm clock and put it back together. But none of his friends were going into those fields, so he did not even consider them. He did not take engineering classes or art design classes in high school or college. To become an architect, he would need to go back to school and take those classes. In our work together, it became clear that he had some talent and an interest in the field of architecture, and if he could do it over, he would go to school to become an architect. After a year of continuing to try to make something else work and continuing to be unhappy with that choice, he decided to go back to school, take the classes he had missed and apply to architecture school. He did that and is very happy about his decision. He really enjoys his classes and is excited about a future in a field that fits his strong interests.

Transitions to a new career might sometimes be made through a portal that is related to the original field. To use law as an example, fields such as professional development for a law firm, higher education administrative work starting out in career services for a law school, marketing for a law firm, public relations, recruiting lawyers either in a corporate setting or law firm setting, financial planning using the contacts made in the field of law and branching out from there, developing of a line of business apparel for professionals, or sales for an entity that services the industry of origin may be possible ways to transition out of the original field and into a new field without fully re-credentialing and going back to school. There are benefits, however, to a full re-credentialing. You learn basics that can help you be successful long-term, and returning to school will help jump-start your relationship building in this new field.

Always try to follow your interests when planning your career moves.

List your strong interests below and rate them on the scale by circling the number that reflects your level of interest; 10 is the highest. The same rating can be used for more than one interest. There is no magic number of interests to include on this list. Some people have only 2 or 3 and others have more than 10.

STRONG INTERESTS WORK SHEET

1. _____ 1 2 3 4 5 6 7 8 9 10

2. _____ 1 2 3 4 5 6 7 8 9 10

3. _____ 1 2 3 4 5 6 7 8 9 10

4. _____ 1 2 3 4 5 6 7 8 9 10

5. _____ 1 2 3 4 5 6 7 8 9 10

6. _____ 1 2 3 4 5 6 7 8 9 10

7. _____ 1 2 3 4 5 6 7 8 9 10

8. _____ 1 2 3 4 5 6 7 8 9 10

9. _____ 1 2 3 4 5 6 7 8 9 10

10. _____ 1 2 3 4 5 6 7 8 9 10

11. _____ 1 2 3 4 5 6 7 8 9 10

12. _____ 1 2 3 4 5 6 7 8 9 10

13. _____ 1 2 3 4 5 6 7 8 9 10

14. _____ 1 2 3 4 5 6 7 8 9 10

STRONG INTERESTS WORK SHEET ILLUSTRATION A

Writing	1 2 3 4 5 6 7 8 ⑨ 10
Counseling, coaching, teaching	1 2 3 4 5 6 7 8 9 ⑩
Making the world a better place	1 2 3 4 5 6 7 8 9 ⑩
Human psychology	1 2 3 4 5 6 7 8 9 ⑩
Interior design	1 2 3 4 5 6 ⑦ 8 9 10
Politics/current events/law	1 2 3 4 5 6 7 ⑧ 9 10
Organizing	1 2 3 4 5 ⑥ 7 8 9 10
The gamesmanship of trial work	1 2 3 4 5 6 7 8 ⑨ 10
Dance and exercise	1 2 3 4 5 6 7 8 ⑨ 10

Above is a partial list of my strong interests. I really love being a career coach and I used to enjoy being a social worker and then a prosecutor. I thought about being a dance instructor and interior designer, but after exploring these fields decided they lacked some of the other elements I needed in a career.

STRONG INTERESTS WORK SHEET ILLUSTRATION B: VIDEO CONTENT PRODUCER

Watching movies	1 2 3 4 5 6 7 8 9 ⑩
Studying movie techniques	1 2 3 4 5 6 7 8 ⑨ 10
Learning about cultural trends	1 2 3 4 5 6 ⑦ 8 9 10
Engaging in wide variety of the arts	1 2 3 4 5 6 ⑦ 8 9 10
Trying new restaurants	1 2 3 4 ⑤ 6 7 8 9 10
Eclectic activities such as cross fit, skating, flying trapeze, music	1 2 3 4 ⑤ 6 7 8 9 10

This is a partial interest list of the video producer from the aptitudes section above.

3. Market Need

If there is not a strong need for workers in the field you are considering, that could mean you would need to be a total standout to be successful, and future jobs could be hard to find. Assess market need by looking at ads and postings, reading local trade journals and newspapers, and talking with people in your field of interest. Always try to be aware of the shifts in market need over time. If you are as innately talented as a Megyn Kelly, then take a shot at broadcast journalism. But if you are not, then stay in the faster current of the workflow. Look for a career that has more opportunities because jobs are plentiful.

4. Skills

Your skills need to match up with the job you seek. If they do not, your chances for getting hired are diminished. To check whether your skills match the workplace requirements, look for postings for jobs in the field you are considering and study the list of required skills. Do you have what the employers are looking for? Is it close? For example, many jobs in the field of communications require a degree in journalism or communications or might be open to skills gained in another field where the experiences are translatable, such as the field of law. It helps to talk with people in the field and learn what they do on a daily basis. Good informational interviews can help you figure out what you need to gain in terms of a viable skillset for the field you are considering.

Find the Intersection of Your AIMS Assessment

Where is the match up of your aptitudes, interests, market need, and your skills? If you do not have the skills you need, how could you get them? Brainstorm with friends, teachers, and family members to try to find the right career direction. If you are stumped, consider taking tests, such as the Strong Interest Inventory or the Highlands Ability Battery. There are many books and articles about these and other tests that can help you uncover or identify your aptitudes and interests. Check with career services at your school to find out about testing services.

Appendix B: AILS Assessment

IF YOU START OFF in the wrong career direction, it can take time and money to reboot, not to mention the emotional toll of that process. It makes the most sense to try to choose the right direction from the start of your career, if at all possible. The AIMS assessment should be coupled with the AILS assessment to be certain you find a personally satisfying career with the likelihood of success in your search efforts. AIMS will tell you where your talents, interests, and the market need indicate you should look. AILS will help you figure out why you are dissatisfied with your career. It can also help you figure out if you are likely to be happy and satisfied in your work-life. Even though there are no guarantees that you will be able to make a perfect match, the likelihood of a good enough match is greater if you use these assessment tools to guide you. In addition, there are some people who are not satisfied with any job or any career. I have worked with some of them. They are pretty grumpy folks and usually can be negative about almost anything. These assessment tools will not overcome that personality problem.

If you have not yet begun your career, use the AILS assessment as a predictive tool to figure out the likelihood of satisfaction with a future career or job. If you are searching for the right area within your field and are currently dissatisfied, use this assessment tool to find the most promising area within your industry.

1. Aptitude

Return to the AIMS assessment and use the aptitude work sheet here.

2. Interest

Return to the AIMS assessment and use the interest work sheet here.

3. Lifestyle

Our work needs to support the lifestyle we want to be happy. Lifestyle includes the amount of money we want to make and the work-life balance equation.

Some people are content to make $40,000, and others will not feel accomplished or safe unless they make far more. There are plenty of people who envision a lifestyle that is sustainable on a compensation level that lies in between these extremes. The lower your salary expectation, the more your career options tend to open up. There are more jobs that pay in a mid-range than there are in a high range. The path to the higher pay scale jobs also tends to involve an outlay of more money to achieve the academic credentials that open the door to those jobs. There are websites like Payscale.com that can help you figure out salary ranges for most careers and jobs. Career services at your high school or university should have information you can access to help you determine pay scales as well.

Lifestyle also includes the issue of balance between work and life outside of work. Many people need a work-life balance that is hard to find in a hard-charging professional environment in a large city. There are many more relaxed work settings, however. Some of these settings are in small towns, others are in government, and others are in companies, trade associations, or not-for-profits. A better match of lifestyle needs to the workplace setting and compensation level can add to career satisfaction. Many people are also willing to put in longer hours if the work they are doing is rewarding and engages their aptitudes and interests.

How do you envision the relationship between your ideal life and your work life? Even if you cannot achieve the best match right away, you can plan for a career that will help you achieve a match in the future. You might need to pay off your student loans by going to a large company or firm where you need to work long hours for a period of time, but your long-term plan could include a move to a small company or small town or a government job after a few years of work. Different settings outside of a large city may have somewhat more reasonable hours and may be less stressful settings. The countervailing factor may be that the work may be less complex, complicated or glamorous, which can be disappointing for some people.

However, if you have a long-range career goal of working closer to a 40- to 50-hour week or having a very flexible or part-time schedule, you will want to enter a field that is likely to permit that career transition in the future, especially once you develop a valuable skill that is in demand. This is really important for people who anticipate wanting to be there when children are young. Many workplaces have been slow to recognize the need for work-life balance and pay little attention to personal needs of employees. Work-life balance is supposed to be the employee's problem. Until there is an economic shift and workers are in demand instead of replaceable, it is imperative to take charge of your career planning and understand the likelihood of eventual flexibility or part-time work in your future career if this matters to you. Look for work-life balance trends in your career of choice. Get the most prestigious credentials you can and earn the most stellar work references you can earn because these can create leverage when you want a more balanced life. Make yourself valuable to the industry you are in. Make sure employers really want your skillset. Plan ahead for your future work-life balance needs.

4. Self-Actualization

Our workplaces shape us. The culture of the workplace, our colleagues, the activities we do to fulfill the requirements for our jobs, the mission we are engaged in, the people we interact with who are our clients and our bosses, the amount of time we spend alone or with others – these and many other elements in the work setting affect the person we are and are becoming.

There is a certain amount of plasticity in people in terms of how we grow as individuals. For example, if you need to pay attention to minute details for your job, you will probably get better at picking up small discrepancies not only at work but outside of work. If you need to be outspoken in a courtroom to be effective, you are likely to become more forceful in your dealings with people generally, even outside of the workplace. If you are a judge or a boss managing a large project or a marital therapist, you not only can but often must, interrupt people, order people to do things to move matters along, and be decisive. We tend to carry our learned behaviors at work into the world at large, including our home and social lives. At work we learn behaviors and are shaped by behaviors that become part of our personalities for better or worse.

In addition, the experiences we have at work with coworkers and bosses, clients, and others, can and often will shape our behavior as well as our view of ourselves. For example, if you are a young professional doing the best you can to learn how to do your job, but you are consistently given negative feedback by your boss, that constant negative interaction might affect your sense of self-worth and self-esteem. Instead of becoming more competent over time, you might become more and more uncertain and even turn into a procrastinator, afraid to begin work on a project for fear it will not turn out well. On the other hand, if the boss is able to convey information with the goal of helping you to do a better job and you are open to that criticism and eager to learn, that interaction could be an extremely positive experience that enhances professional development. It is that mixture of who you are and the environment you are working in, plus the people you work with most closely that can deeply affect your satisfaction at work.

Every workplace is a unique mixture of people, workplace culture, overarching mission, and work that needs to be done. The people who work in that particular setting will be affected by that particular environment. To make matters more complex, however, every person is also unique. Two people in the very same workplace can and will react very differently to events and situations. For example, a woman working in a small office with a number of men who tell dirty jokes and laugh about their sexual exploits might well experience that workplace as offensive and even intolerable. She might have actionable grounds for a harassment lawsuit. But another woman joining that same group might feel comfortable talking and laughing about her own sexual exploits. She might find the workplace to be not only tolerable, but collegial and lots of fun. People are unique and will experience the same place very differently. We really need to be aware of personal differences in sensibilities and sensitivities, including our own.

What this means for you as you try to find right career direction is that you want to figure out for yourself how your workplace is affecting you. Given who you are, what is happening to you? And would this be likely to happen at other workplaces doing the same kind of work? Or is this workplace idiosyncratic? This can be difficult to figure out.

If you are someone who values honesty and prides yourself on being ethical, but your job calls for you to engage in devious tactics or hide the truth, that is probably affecting you in a negative way. This kind of workplace culture will not make you happy.

If you are a team-oriented person who loves interaction with others but your job or career requires that you spend 90% of your time alone in front of a computer doing research, and no one in the office says hello or smiles or talks with you, that will affect you in a negative way. Is there something else in the work you do that counterbalances that negative culture?

If you are working in a place where you are valued and listened to, your opinion matters, and you have developed some expertise, you are probably becoming more confident not only as a worker, but as a person outside of work. You want to try to keep working at a place like this, all things being equal.

How is your workplace shaping you? How are you responding to the people and the work you are doing? Do you like the person you are becoming? What is working for you? What is not working for you?

Use the exercise on the next page to write down the ways the workplace is hurting you and/or helping you become the person you want to be by identifying your goals and then assessing the effect of your workplace on the achievement of your goals. Write down whether your job is helping or hurting your ability to be the person you want to be.

GOALS WORK SHEET

1. _____

Hurting?

Helping?

2. _____

Hurting?

Helping?

3. _____

Hurting?

Helping?

4. _____

Hurting?

Helping?

5. _____

Hurting?

Helping?

6. _____

Hurting?

Helping?

Figure Out What AILS You or Creates Dissatisfaction in Your Career

Now that you have done this exercise, take a minute to review what you have learned. How closely matched are your aptitudes, interests, lifestyle needs, and personal goals with your current career/job? Overall, are you well-matched for your current career/job? If you have at least some satisfaction in all four categories – aptitude, interest, lifestyle, and self-actualization – you are likely to have a reasonably satisfying career or job. If one or more of these categories is missing the mark for you, you may need to work on changing the job or the career or your responsibilities, adding more of one kind of work and doing less of the sort of work you do not do as well or have less of an interest in doing. This exercise can start to help you figure out what you need to shift or tweak.

If, on the other hand, you are totally lacking one or more of these basic elements of career satisfaction, it is likely that you are dissatisfied with your career, and unless you change your field or industry, your workplace, the type of job you do, or another key component of your work situation, you will be likely to continue to experience your work life in a negative way.

Many people who are missing one or more of these four elements of career satisfaction are wearing out their loved ones by complaining about how unhappy they are. This exercise can help you at least start to identify where the dissatisfaction is coming from. If you have determined there is a serious disconnect between what you need from your career or job and what you are getting, do the Essential Elements Assessment to identify what would be a better career or job for you.

The next exercise, Essential Elements, will help you to more closely identify and hone a career direction that will be a better fit.

Appendix C: Essential Elements

You SHOULD DO the Essential Elements assessment if one of the following describes your situation:

1. You do not enjoy your current job/career and want to find a better fit.
2. You have more than one choice of job and you want to check to be sure you are choosing a job that matches your needs reasonably well.
3. You are starting a job search, and you want to make sure you are looking for a job that suits your needs reasonably well.

Who does not need to do the Essential Elements exercise:

Anyone who already knows that his current job/career is working well for him and is conducting a job search for the same kind of job that he had before does not need to do the Essential Elements exercise.

What Is the Essential Elements Exercise?

Every person has a unique set of building blocks or elements that helps him have a satisfying career and enjoy his work-life. These building blocks are such things as a need for a mission that motivates you, control over your hours, a collegial group and a team approach to work, and many others. These elements will be different for each person. If you can identify what you need from your job, you will be in a better position to conduct a job search for a position that will meet your unique needs. This exercise helps you identify the building blocks of a career that will be more sustaining for you by creating a template for a job that works well for you personally. Once you have this template, you can vet your potential job or career for your needs, and you will be more likely to find work that will satisfy you and in which you will excel.

The Essential Elements exercise starts with a work history to figure out what your particular building blocks are.

Work History

List work you have done, paid or unpaid, whether or not it was termed a "job." Include internships, work you did for fundraising events, and volunteer work of any kind, and include college and professional school on the list of work you have done.

Under each work entry make a list of what you liked and did not like about the work. Include your reaction to the people, the hours, the type of work you did, and anything else about the job or work that stands out in your mind. Ask yourself "what could have been changed about this job to make it better for me?" In other words, pretend you are going to fix this job so that it would be a good one for you. What would be different? This is a good way to identify your building blocks.

It is important to assess every position you have ever had whether they were paid or unpaid jobs, but you can lump early jobs together. For example, if you had many waitressing jobs or camp counselor jobs and your experiences in each instance were similar, you can group them under one heading.

WORK HISTORY WORK SHEET

Job 1: _____

Liked:

Disliked:

Job 2: _____

Liked:

Disliked:

Job 3: _____

Liked:

Disliked:

Job 4: _____

Liked:

Disliked:

Job 5: _____

Liked:

Disliked:

WORK HISTORY ILLUSTRATION

Job: Working at Joe's Fish Place as a server in high school

Liked

Loved the people I worked with – blue collar, salt-of-the earth guys
Great customers – friendly and talkative
Hours were good
When work was over I was done
I didn't take work home with me

Disliked

The pay was too low
The work was stressful when we got very busy
Work was too menial to do this job for long
Didn't use my mind or feel challenged

Job: Project Assistant for small personal injury firm

Liked

Liked research and writing a lot
Really respected and liked the lawyers I worked for
I knew what I was supposed to do
I didn't bring work home at night

Disliked

Work was boring
Did not get to interact with clients
The mission of plaintiff's personal injury cases wasn't right for me

Job: College

Liked

Loved college!
Independence
Learning new things
Great people
Some terrific professors

Great parties and social life
Relaxed atmosphere mostly

Disliked
Studying for exams was very stressful

Job: Residential Assistant in college

Liked
Liked counseling the students a lot
Enjoyed the independence
I like it when I could help someone handle tough situation

Disliked
Role of policeman
Lack of guidance about how to handle tough situations

Job: Campus Newspaper – getting and writing up stories

Liked
Really enjoyed hearing people's stories
Loved seeing my work in print – product was cool
When we finished the paper we were done and didn't take work
 home

Disliked
Deadline stress
Low pay
Office politics about who got the good stories

Job: Law School

Liked
Some of the people were nice
Liked learning new ideas and concepts

Disliked
Hated law school! Even though I did well
Hated the competitive people

Hated the Socratic method

Hated studying the law and did not know how to do it well until the third year

Job: Large Law Firm Litigation Associate

Liked

Liked the partner I worked with most closely

Enjoyed learning new concepts

Liked the money

Disliked

Didn't like the mission of litigating or getting more money for rich people or companies

Hated the stress

Hated having to work when my disorganized partner gave me a job to do at the last minute

Not enough mentoring

Not sure what I was doing

Lack of structure made me crazy

Did not get to work with clients

Felt isolated working behind closed doors doing research

Work History Analysis

What emerges from this work history are the following themes:

1. Enjoys *learning new things*
2. Enjoys *structured setting* with clear information about what to do
3. Likes to interact with people in a *team/collegial* setting
4. Wants to make enough *money* to feel secure
5. Likes personal interaction; needs to *interact with people* as part of the job
6. Likes the *role of helping*, giving advice, teaching, guiding others
7. Needs to *avoid excessive stress*
8. Prefers *projects that end* so that work does not spill over to life

outside of work
9. Likes to be *trusted* by the boss
10. Prefers a more *relaxed pace*
11. Needs to have a *mission* that he feels is worthwhile
12. Needs to *avoid isolation*

Once you identify the major themes, you have the elements that make up Essential Elements. You can create a list of the elements you need to have to be satisfied with your work, and create a list of elements you need to avoid to be satisfied with your work. Review the illustrations given here and then use the worksheets at the end to create and rate your own lists.

ESSENTIAL ELEMENTS ILLUSTRATION

Using the work history illustration and analysis example above, here is a list of essential elements for this person to seek out in the job search.

Essential Elements to Achieve in Work Life/Needs to Have in Career:
1. Uptick on the learning curve – learn new things on the job
2. Structure and clear definition of expectations
3. Team, collegial culture
4. Enough money to feel secure: at least $_____
5. Interactive role involving people as part of the job
6. The role of the helping person, teacher, guide, counselor
7. Projects that end, finality
8. Trusted to do the job
9. Mission that matters (to him)
10. Casual, relaxed pace
11. Mentoring

Here is a list of what this person should try to avoid.

Irritants to Avoid
1. High stress workplace

2. Fast pace
3. Isolation
4. Boredom
5. Lack of trust
6. Lack of structure
7. Lack of mentoring
8. Low pay
9. Projects that go on and on with no end in sight
10. Mission that does not matter to him

Try to put only the most irritating elements on the irritants list – the ones you feel "allergic" to – for example, the "micromanager" boss, isolation, the "screamer" boss, the backbiting coworkers, or lack of control over your free time because of last-minute assignments. These are elements that drive some people crazy. Every person has his own unique list. The work history is a chance to think through these irritants to avoid those that are particularly annoying for you.

In some cases, you may not have enough work experience to know what your hot buttons are, or, for that matter, to know what you absolutely have to have in your work life to be happy. The work history is a more useful vehicle for people who have had at least some work experience. The work history is also a work in progress. Some elements will be added or taken off the list as a work life evolves over the course of a career.

The themes that emerge in this exercise will usually continue to reappear throughout a person's work life. In some cases, however, the theme will become less salient over time. For example, a person who wants to have control over handling matters, interacting with clients, and being trusted to do the work will, in fact, grow into that role over time. If this person keeps working hard, eventually he will become the boss who does have client contact and who is fully trusted to do the work. The work history is a snapshot of current work desires.

Note that every person has a different idea about what matters and what does not matter when it comes to the mission. For one person, helping companies be successful is a perfectly good mission. For another person, the mission has to be about helping poor people, helping women and children, or trying to make the world a better place.

This determination is idiosyncratic and personal. There are other missions as well. What one person seeks may not resonate with another person. I have counseled people who wanted to be sure that Libertarian values were represented in Congress and felt strongly about that goal, while another person I counseled at the same time was working tirelessly to be sure that Libertarian values were not represented in Congress.

Now that you have a list of Essential Elements, you should grade each one on a scale of 1 to 10 to reflect how much this element matters to you.

If you give an element a "10" (the highest need), then you should not take a job if you will have to do without this element in the workplace. As you rate each element, ask yourself these questions:

"How much do I have to have this in my work life?"

"How much am I willing to 'give a little' on this?"

If you give an element something lower than a "5," it may not be important enough for you to keep on the list.

After you finish grading each Essential Element, then grade your list of Irritants to Avoid. When you are assessing your irritants, you are grading them on a scale of 1 to 10, with "10" reflecting your highest level of hate and irritation. As you go through your list of irritants, ask yourself these questions:

"How much do I hate this on a scale of 1 to 10?"

"How much am I willing to 'give a little' on this?"

See the sample of completed Essential Elements and Irritants to Avoid.

This exercise helps you assess your level of dissatisfaction. If there is a severe mismatch between what someone needs in her work life and what she is getting on the job, that person may need to conduct a job search for a better fitting job or career.

ESSENTIAL ELEMENTS SAMPLE

Here is a list of what this person gave as a grade for each essential element. (*How much do you need this on a scale of 1-10, with 10 the highest?*)

Essential Elements to Have in Work Life

1. Uptick on the learning curve – learn new things on the job — 1 2 3 4 5 6 7 (8) 9 10
2. Structure and clear definition of expectations — 1 2 3 4 5 6 (7) 8 9 10
3. Team, collegial culture — 1 2 3 4 5 6 7 8 (9) 10
4. Enough money to feel secure: at least $_____ — 1 2 3 4 5 6 (7) 8 9 10
5. Interactive role involving people as part of the job — 1 2 3 4 5 6 7 8 (9) 10
6. The role of the helping person, teacher, guide, counselor — 1 2 3 4 5 6 7 8 9 (10)
7. Projects that end; finality — 1 2 3 4 5 6 7 (8) 9 10
8. Trusted to do the job — 1 2 3 4 5 6 (7) 8 9 10
9. Mission that matters (to him) — 1 2 3 4 5 6 7 8 9 (10)
10. Casual, relaxed pace — 1 2 3 4 5 6 7 (8) 9 10
11. Mentoring — 1 2 3 4 5 6 7 (8) 9 10

Here is a list of what this person gave as a grade for each irritant to avoid. *(How much do you hate this on a scale of 1-10, with 10 the highest?)*

Irritants to Avoid

1. High-stress workplace — 1 2 3 4 5 6 7 8 (9) 10
2. Fast pace — 1 2 3 4 5 6 7 8 (9) 10
3. Isolation — 1 2 3 4 5 6 7 8 9 (10)
4. Boredom — 1 2 3 4 5 6 (7) 8 9 10
5. Lack of trust — 1 2 3 4 5 (6) 7 8 9 10
6. Lack of structure — 1 2 3 4 5 (6) 7 8 9 10
7. Lack of mentoring — 1 2 3 4 5 6 7 8 (9) 10
8. Low pay — 1 2 3 4 5 6 (7) 8 9 10
9. Projects that go on and on with no end in sight — 1 2 3 4 5 6 7 8 (9) 10
10. Mission that does not matter to him — 1 2 3 4 5 6 7 8 9 (10)

If you follow these instructions, you can create a template for the type of job that would work well for you. We know no job is perfect, but if you can try to get many of these elements into your work life, you will be happier. Additionally, if you can avoid or minimize exposure to elements you hate, you will be happier.

ESSENTIAL ELEMENTS WORK SHEET

(How much I need this element on a scale of 1-10 with, 10 the highest.)

1. _____ 1 2 3 4 5 6 7 8 9 10

2. _____ 1 2 3 4 5 6 7 8 9 10

3. _____ 1 2 3 4 5 6 7 8 9 10

4. _____ 1 2 3 4 5 6 7 8 9 10

5. _____ 1 2 3 4 5 6 7 8 9 10

6. _____ 1 2 3 4 5 6 7 8 9 10

7. _____ 1 2 3 4 5 6 7 8 9 10

8. _____ 1 2 3 4 5 6 7 8 9 10

9. _____ 1 2 3 4 5 6 7 8 9 10

10. _____ 1 2 3 4 5 6 7 8 9 10

IRRITANTS TO AVOID WORK SHEET

(How much I hate this element on a scale of 1-10, with 10 the highest.)

1. _____ 1 2 3 4 5 6 7 8 9 10

2. _____ 1 2 3 4 5 6 7 8 9 10

3. _____ 1 2 3 4 5 6 7 8 9 10

4. _____ 1 2 3 4 5 6 7 8 9 10

5. _____ 1 2 3 4 5 6 7 8 9 10

6. _____ 1 2 3 4 5 6 7 8 9 10

7. _____ 1 2 3 4 5 6 7 8 9 10

8. _____ 1 2 3 4 5 6 7 8 9 10

9. _____ 1 2 3 4 5 6 7 8 9 10

10. _____ 1 2 3 4 5 6 7 8 9 10

If you are dissatisfied with your current work situation, you can use the work sheets to assess your current job to see why you are not satisfied.

Use a different colored pen for this exercise. Go through each element and evaluate your current workplace. You are grading your workplace against your worksheets to see how it is doing in terms of *your needs*. For example, if you need to learn new things and you graded that an "8," and your job gives you that uptick on the learning curve you want, then put a colored dot about the "8" you circled. The job is meeting your needs on that score. If your job is only giving you a "2" or a "3" then it is falling short of your needs.

Look for serious mismatches between your wished-for elements and the job you currently have. Any time there is a mismatch of 4 or more points, that should be considered serious.

For example, if you need the role of the helping person and you have given that a "10," and your current job gets a grade of "2" or "3," then you have a serious mismatch between what you need and what you are getting. This is one of the reasons you are not satisfied with your job.

What if you need a "Mission that Matters to me" and you give that a "10" but you grade your current job at a "1"? That is a mismatch of 9 points. Here is another serious mismatch of your aspirations and needs with a job that is not meeting those needs.

Whenever you have a serious mismatch of a deeply felt need with a job that is flunking your needs, you have the seeds for career or job dissatisfaction. If you have even one of these mismatches, you are likely to be dissatisfied until and unless you can find work that is a better match, change your role within the workplace, or find opportunities to meet that need outside of work and have the time to engage in them. You want to develop a career plan to eventually meet that need.

If you have only slight mismatches between your worksheet needs and the current job you are doing, you probably can hang in there and keep your current job to put bread on the table, while conducting a quest for a workplace or career direction that is an even better fit.

Next, grade your current workplace using the Irritants to Avoid worksheet. Are you able to avoid high stress? You are looking for a "9" – how is your workplace doing on this score?

You really hate isolation. You give that a "10" on the hate scale. How much are you able to avoid isolation at your job?

If you have a very high level of irritation and an inability to avoid the irritants that you really hate, you have a serious problem in terms of matching up your deeply felt needs to the reality of your job. You will need to look for a new job or an altered culture at work unless there is some other way to avoid the things you cannot stand.

You can also use your worksheets to vet future job opportunities. When you have located an opportunity that you think could be good for you, go back to your worksheets and think about whether this job is going to meet your needs.

If you gave the role of the helping person a "10," are you likely to get that?

If you gave feeling good about the mission a "10," will you feel that way about this job?

If you gave interacting with people a "9," will that be part of your work life?

How can you figure out if you will get what you need from a potential job? Your networking effort is the key to learning this information. LinkedIn is a valuable tool.

As you make your way on your quest, meeting with and talking with the people who have on-the-ground information about the workplace you are vetting, you can ask questions that help you to learn what you need to know.

> "What is Chris like as a boss? Is he a micromanager? Is he a screamer? Disorganized? Does he trust his co-workers to do the job?"

> "What kind of work pace do people have over there? Do they bring work home at night and over the weekends?"

If you talk with people in confidence, you can get information that is helpful to you to figure out if this work setting will be closer to your needs. One good way to learn this information is to find people who have recently left the workplace (within the past year or two), and call them up and ask if they would be willing to talk with you. It sounds like this:

> "I am considering taking a job at the firm you worked at two years ago. I was wondering if you would be willing

to talk with me in absolute confidence about your experiences over there. I just want to be sure I will be able to obtain what I am looking for if I take this job."

How do you find people who have left that workplace? LinkedIn is a valuable resource for this information. Use LinkedIn and try to meet in person or by phone or via the Internet if an in-person meeting is not possible. Search for people who have worked at these places you are interested in to learn more about the workplaces so you can make educated guesses about the likelihood your needs will be met.

Another source of this kind of information is anyone who is loosely affiliated with the workplace, such as spouses or friends of people who are or have been working at the workplace you are trying to vet.

Conclusion

The value of these exercises lies in the understanding you gain from identifying the elements you need for a satisfying career. When you are developing relationships and seeking opportunities, people will ask you what you want from your career. You need to know what you want. When you interview for a job, the interviewers will ask you what your long-term plan is for your career. You need to be able to articulate that. If you are not happy with your career, you need to understand why that is and have an idea about what would make you happier.

Even though no job is perfect, some are better than others. When we know ourselves well enough to know what we are looking for, and understand the work settings that will bring out the best in us, we will have more productive and effective job searches, and more productive and satisfying work lives.

Appendix D: The "Basket of Skills" or Skills-Based Résumé

MANY JOB SEEKERS prepare a chronological résumé. There is nothing wrong with that. That type of résumé highlights longevity at one workplace, a consistent job history, and loyalty.

In a relationship-building search, however, the job seeker is meeting in person with many people. The idea of an in-person meeting is to show up for a breakfast, lunch, dinner, or coffee, or by invitation at the contact person's office, and have a conversation that opens doors.

There is a lot of information that a job seeker is trying to talk about with the contact person. In fact, it may be difficult to cover all of the topics that she wants to try to cover in the time frame of a lunch or a cup of coffee.

For that reason, it is important to prepare a résumé for purposes of the in-person meeting that makes it very easy for the contact person to grasp your background immediately. The "skills-based" résumé does a good job of that.

As illustrated on the following pages, a skills-based résumé or "basket of skills" style résumé has a skills summary at the top of the résumé. That summary can be altered depending on the contact person you are meeting with. The skills summary should highlight the core competencies that match up with the contact person's likely connections for you.

See the next page for a sample of a skills-based résumé. The new graduate, without a lengthy work history, will usually do better to start the résumé with education, highlighting academic successes, honors, leadership experiences, and other indicators of future success. Internships and work experiences follow in the next section of the résumé. Some new graduates will opt for a "Objectives" or "Goals" section at the top of the résumé, but that is probably not necessary if you are meeting in person and can clearly articulate what you are looking for with the contact.

Your name
Your home address
Your phone number
Your e-mail address

SKILLS SUMMARY

[Start with your current skills, and highlight your area(s) of expertise.
This shows what you can do for the employer without further training. Quantify results.
Use numbers to help the reader understand your skill level.]

Income partner with eight years of litigation and regulatory experience. Responsibilities include counseling, drafting motions and briefs, taking over 30 depositions, preparing pretrial memoranda, participating as lead attorney in over 40 regulatory hearings, legal research and writing, analyzing and drafting legislation, managing large document reviews including associate oversight in complex litigation matters.

EXPERIENCE

[Next, tell the reader in brief form where you have worked,
when you were there, and your role at that job.]

Firm A LLP, Chicago, Illinois
Associate, Commercial Litigation, 2000–Present; Summer Associate, 1999

Firm B LLP, Chicago, Illinois
Summer Associate, 1998

EDUCATION

[Next, tell the reader your education, including honors you earned.]

University of Illinois College of Law. J.D. *with distinction* 1996, Law Review Notes Editor, Research Assistant for Prof. —— on regulatory issues and sustainable energy, co-author of "——".

Bradley University B.S. Psychology, *cum laude*, 1993

[Next, list professional publications, memberships, community involvement, and interests, especially if the interests are ones that might open the door to a conversation with your contact person, such as a shared interest or unusual pursuit. Try to keep all of this on one page.]

[You can also have a second page of Professional Accomplishments that briefly describe in bulleted form your significant achievements. These can be talking points for your meeting.]

Appendix E: The Master Lists of People and Places

THE FOCUS OF your networking meetings should be on learning what is happening in the neighborhood(s) you think you want to join, and what is going on in the villages behind the castles you want to be a part of.

To that end, your conversations with knights and wizards should focus at least in part on the places you are finding out about that could be good matches for you, and the other people in the neighborhood doing the work you think you want to do.

The Master List of People and Places should grow as you learn more about your targeted neighborhoods.

The way to create a Master List is to simply list every person you know about or have learned about in your online and interpersonal research that you want to meet up with. On another page list every workplace you would like to learn more about. You keep growing these lists as your knowledge grows. Every time you go to a relationship-building meeting, print off the list and bring it to the meeting.

At the meeting, pull out your lists and do the following:

- Ask your contact person to review the list of people and check off people he knows and ask if this person is someone who is "nice" or "friendly" or "helpful" and would be open to talking with you to learn more about the market in general and specific workplaces.
- If appropriate, ask if he would be willing to send an e-mail on your behalf to that person to help you learn more about the field, neighborhood, realm.
- You also want to ask your contact person to review the list of places that you think could be a good match for you and add to the list.
- Then ask him what, if anything, he has heard about the

places where he knows people and whether he has heard if any of these places are busy, active, and growing, and have a good reputation, meaning people like to work there. You are looking for useful gossip, on-the-ground information, and market knowledge.

Another way to create useful Master Lists of people and places is to use the format on the following page. In these Master Lists, the networker has figured out the castles of interest, and is filling in the key keepers, the knights, and the wizards and is keeping notes about her progress.

Castles	Key Keepers	Knights/ Wizards	Notes

Appendix F: Checklist and Guide for Your Job Quest

1. DO ASSESSMENT WORK IF YOU NEED TO LEARN MORE ABOUT YOURSELF

Are you looking for your first job or are you looking for a better career direction?

If so, do exercises that help you **find your career "sweet spot"**:

A. **AIMS**: *Aptitude, Interest, Market Need, Skillset*
B. **AILS**: *Aptitude, Interest, Lifestyle, Self-Actualization*
C. **Essential Elements**

If you like your career direction and want the same type of job you have currently, you may skip over the "sweet spot" exercises and go directly to 2. QUEST PREPARATION CHECKLIST.

2. QUEST PREPARATION CHECKLIST

+ Create a **basket of skills** résumé
+ Locate the **work-flow**
+ Create a **master list of people and places**
+ Know the **formula for landing jobs**
+ Articulate your **dream and dilemma**
+ Be prepared for your **interview** before you set out

If you are feeling upset or depressed:

+ Do a **mental status check** before you set out
+ Get **support** or **help** if you need it

3. GUIDING PRINCIPLES FOR THE QUEST

- Start your quest with close friends (knights/wizards)
- Meet with people suggested by your knights/wizards
- Try to meet more villagers in the right neighborhood by going to conferences, meetings, and other places frequented by that group
- Meet in person as much as possible
- Breakfast, lunch, dinner, or coffee
- Expand your encounters with knights/wizards everywhere

    Use the **starter conversation** to open up relationship potential

    Avoid the "J" word when you start out

    Try to have long, gossipy, rumor-filled conversations to learn more

    Use the **voice test** to find natural counselors

    The voice of the natural counselor goes up

    Be open and engaging, creative and bold

    But not aggressive or a pest

    Cultivate lucky attitudes:

    Interaction

    Optimism

    Pragmatism

    Intuition

    Tenacity

    Opportunism

    Generosity

    Create a virtual round table by asking helpful people to join it. Consult the knights and wizards of your roundtable when you question your judgment or need help

- Look for **treasure chest** people

    You never know. . . .

- Use **opportunism** to enhance your luck
  - *Adventurous attitude*
  - *Good research*
  - *Connections with key people*
- Engineer meetings with key people
  - *Be careful to conform to workplace practices*
  - *Never be a pest or aggressive or a fraud*

4. GUIDING PRINCIPLES FOR IN-PERSON MEETINGS

In conversations with knights and wizards, follow these principles:

- Create a **zone of comfort** first
  - *Friendship lite*
  - *Trust relationships are created by listening and giving back*
- Discuss your contact's **biography**
  - *. . . but do not get stuck on that topic*
- Tell your knights/wizards your **dream and dilemma or goal and problem**
  - *Describe your goal*
  - *Explain your problem*
- Focus the conversation on your **Master List**
  - *People doing the work you want to be doing*
  - *Places or castles you seek*
- Learn the on-the-ground information:
  - *Gossip (what is happening in the village)*
  - *Work-flow (busy, active, growing work places)*
  - *Culture of the place (people like to work there)*
  - *Try to learn the keeper of the keys*
- Give your knights/wizards clear **prototypes**
  - *Illustrations of castles you are seeking*

> *Use Master Lists of People and Places to brainstorm with people you meet with*

+ Find more **nice people** in the village to learn from

    Everyone knows who is nice and who is not

5. DO GOOD DEEDS

+ Give back to your knights and wizards

    Create a positive buzz

+ Give gifts or good deeds

    A gift of attention

    A gift of information

    A gift of promotion

    A gift of connection

    Volunteered help

    A more tangible gift

6. ONCE YOU KNOW A LIKELY CASTLE, YOU REACH A TIPPING POINT: MOVE FROM QUEST TO CAMPAIGN WITH RESPECT TO THAT CASTLE

In your campaign to be hired, follow these principles:

+ Use the formula for landing jobs to know if you are at the tipping point

    Your skill set matches the needs of the workplace

    The work-flow is there

    The culture is likely to be a good fit

    You try to come to their attention through a trusted contact

+ Ask for endorsement if the elements are there

    Your contact knows you, likes you, knows your work and work ethic

Your contact knows someone on the castle staff who is respected or a gatekeeper

There could be a need for help at this castle

- Seek out villagers and others who could help you find the keeper of the keys or meet other staff

  Keep developing trust relationships

7. REACH THE GOALS OF YOUR JOB QUEST

- Find and meet the key keepers and have an excellent interview

- Create a supportive network of knights and wizards who will help and sustain you for your entire career

- Land the job you want

Works Cited

Beatty, Kimberly. "The Math Behind the Networking Claim." *Jobfully Online Content and Marketing*. (blog)
http://blog.jobfully.com/2010/07/the-math-behind-the-networking-claim/

Cappelli, Peter. *Why Good People Can't Get Jobs*. Philadelphia: Wharton Digital Press, 2012

Crispin, Gerry. "Source of Hire Report." *CareerXroads*.
http://www.careerxroads.com/news/articles.asp

Dominus, Susan. "The Saintly Way to Succeed." *New York Times Sunday Magazine*.
http://www.nytimes.com/2013/03/31/magazine/is-giving-the-secret-to-getting-ahead.html

Smith, Jacquelyn. "7 Things You Probably Didn't Know About Your Job Search." *Forbes Online*.
http://www.forbes.com/sites/jacquelynsmith/2013/04/17/7-things-you-probably-didnt-know-about-your-job-search/

Smith, Jacquelyn. "New Research Shows Where Employers Find Their New Hires." *Forbes Online*.
http://www.forbes.com/sites/jacquelynsmith/2012/04/06/new-research-shows-where-employers-find-their-new-hires/

Wiseman, Richard. *The Luck Factor: The Four Essential Principles*. New York: Hyperion Books, 2003.

Made in the USA
Lexington, KY
08 February 2018